The Zulu War

A West Country man, David Clammer teaches in a
large comprehensive school and specialises in remedial
education. He had written no books before *The Zulu
War* but has since written *The Victorian Army in
Pictures*. Of *The Zulu War* he says 'My sole qualification
for writing this book was enthusiasm.'

D1384807

David Clammer

The Zulu War

Pan Books London and Sydney

First published 1973 by David & Charles (Holdings) Ltd
This edition published 1975 by Pan Books Ltd,
Cavaye Place, London SW10 9PG
© David George Clammer 1973

ISBN 0 330 24582 1

Made and printed in Great Britain by
Hazell Watson & Viney Ltd, Aylesbury, Bucks

Contents

List of plates

List of maps

Acknowledgements

I wish to acknowledge the assistance given me by the
interlibrary loan service, and especially the Yatton branch
of the Somerset County Library; the library of the War Office
(Army); the proprietors of the *Illustrated London News*; the
Radio Times Hulton Picture Library; and John Murray
(Publishers) Ltd for permission to quote from General
Sir H. Smith-Dorrien's *Memories of Forty-Eight Years'
Service*. I also wish to thank Mrs Purdon for the care
she took in typing the manuscript.

for Liz

Chapter one
The Way to War

Queen Victoria's long reign was constantly disturbed by the almost ceaseless warfare that flared along the ever extending frontiers of the Empire: the inevitable concomitant of imperialism. The Army enjoyed little respite from campaigns and punitive expeditions, for sometimes two or even three of these frontier wars were waged within a single year. With the exception of the Crimean War, all were 'native wars', and their causes were as various as the opponents they presented were diverse. They were fought to repel or punish incursions into British territory; to quell insurrections; to suppress barbarism; to enforce trade and diplomatic agreements; to assert imperial prestige; to humble contumacious despots; or very often for a combination of such reasons. The Zulu War came about for several of these reasons, and for one other besides: it was a war launched by a British colony in self-defence, on the principle that the best form of defence is attack. Today, it would be called a pre-emptive strike; to its critics at the time, it was a war of aggression. The origins of the British invasion of Zululand were three-fold: the policy of South African confederation, the history and the unique standing of the Zulu nation, and the personality of the governor-general.

As Victoria's reign lengthened, the vast and sprawling Empire continued to expand, not so much by the deliberate policy of successive British governments, which were often reluctant to assume fresh territorial and financial responsibilities, but by what undoubtedly seemed to many at the time to be a spontaneous, if haphazard, natural growth. The continuous growth in the area and population of the Empire, as diverse racially as it was widespread geographically, brought British governments enormous and costly problems in terms of administration, native policy and defence; and by the 1860s the answer to these difficulties seemed to be confederation: the establishment of the white colonies as virtual self-governing nation-states, largely responsible for their own internal policies and bearing the cost of their own defence. The arrangement was mutually advantageous. The colonies secured a large measure of self-determination, while having the Mother Country to guarantee their integrity; Britain, relieved of vast expense, had the satisfaction of seeing the colonies crystallise into a more coherent and stronger formation – a Greater Britain.

By 1870 the experiment was working well in Australia and New Zealand, from which all British troops had been withdrawn, and in Canada, where the only redcoats left were those of the garrison at the naval base at Halifax. South Africa seemed overripe for the same step, and in 1874 Disraeli's Secretary of State for the Colonies, the Earl of Carnarvon, decided that the time had come to take it.

Carnarvon enumerated the advantages of confederation to the Cabinet. The flow of European immigrants and money into southern Africa would be increased, resulting in greater stability and prosperity. Demands for imperial troops would be much less probable, and administrative costs would be reduced. But above all, confederation would facilitate the establishment of a humane and unified native policy without which long-term peace, prosperity and political stability were impossible.

South Africa, however, presented a chaotic spectacle, and even without the antipathy that subsisted between the several territories which Carnarvon proposed to unite, the task would have been tremendous.

Cape Colony was the largest and strongest of these territories, having its own parliament and prime minister, in addition to a governor. It enjoyed some of the benefits of civilisation, including theoretical racial equality, but was split into two provinces, western and eastern, the latter wishing to break away from the other entirely. Beyond the frontier of the Eastern Province lay unlikely sounding places such as Fingoland and Mpondoland To the north of the Orange River, and beyond the Vaal, lay the Boer republics, the Orange Free State and the Transvaal, thinly populated by the Dutch who had quit the Cape during the Great Trek. The Boers carried their personal independence to

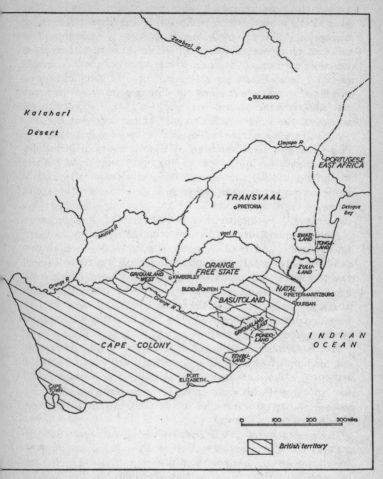

South Africa at the time of the Zulu War

the point where their own democratic institutions had broken down. Both countries were insolvent, and in 1876 a disastrous attempt on the part of a commando to storm the stronghold of a Basuto chief named Sekukuni led to fears that they were incapable even of self-defence. The frontiers of the Transvaal, moreover, where they marched with those of Zululand, were ill-defined, giving rise to a long standing dispute over what came to be known as the 'Disputed Territories'. It looked very much as though the Boer republics could at any moment become involved in a large scale native war, or dissolve into anarchy. The situation was complicated by the discovery of diamonds at Kimberley in the 1870s resulting in large scale British immigration. There remained Natal, a colony ruled by a lieutenant-governor, and enjoying a large measure of autonomy.

Carnarvon's preliminary moves towards confederation came to nothing. The Boers would never voluntarily surrender their independence, and J. C. Molteno, the Prime Minister of the Cape, proved equally intractable. The secretary of state decided therefore to call a conference to discuss the issue, which convened in London in August 1876, with Carnarvon in the chair. It was not a success. The Transvaal and Natal were not represented; President Brand attended on behalf of the Orange Free State, but quickly walked out; and Molteno, in London on quite separate business, declined to appear at all. Carnarvon and his policy had reached an impasse, from which he could see only one way out – he would send out a new governor to the Cape, armed with wide terms of reference and discretionary powers, and see if some kind of unity could not be imposed upon South Africa that way.

The new Governor, Sir Henry Bartle Edward Frere, landed at Cape Town in April 1877. Carnarvon's choice was impressive. Frere was an imperial administrator of vast experience, with a distinguished career in India behind him. The post of governor-general of the Cape held few attractions for a man in his position, especially as he was on the point of retirement, yet Frere consented to take the position because of his profound belief in the civilising mission of Britain, and because to lead a notoriously intractable land towards the harmony of confederation would, if successful, be a fitting achievement with which to crown his life's work.

In August, Frere visited Natal and did not like what he saw. The situation in the colony reminded him of nothing so much as the build-up of unrest and disaffection which had preceded the Mutiny in India – in which he had participated with distinction – and it became apparent to him, as it already was to Carnarvon, that a settlement of the native question was the key to stability in southern Africa.

The state of affairs in Natal was indeed perilous. Out of 12 million acres, only 2 million were owned by some 300,000 natives, while 20,000 Europeans owned most of the rest. Over-crowding had been further increased by land speculators. Much of the land was of poor quality and was becoming even less productive through overgrazing caused by an excess of the live-stock by which the Bantu measured their wealth. Wood was in short supply as a result of deforestation, in consequence of which dung was burned as fuel, so impoverishing the land still further. Such an economy produced little surplus except labour, and vast numbers of the Kaffirs were already dependent upon wages, often paid by the more unscrupulous whites in the form of guns. As long as conditions remained fairly normal, the real position of the natives was concealed, but it was clear to Frere that the frail structure of their economy could not withstand a heavy blow.

The blow was not long in falling. In 1877 a vast area of the Transvaal, Natal and Zululand was afflicted by a serious drought, which became more serious as it continued into 1878. The movement of the tribes in search of pasturage occasioned by this gave rise to a devastating epidemic of lung-sickness amongst their cattle.

In October 1877, the Ninth Kaffir War erupted, but was soon extinguished. To Frere, it seemed evident, however, that the day of isolated wars was passing. Kaffirs, Zulus, Fingos, Swazis, Mashonas and Griquas, all were slowly coalescing under white pressure, and it seemed to require only a spark to kindle the flame of a general war against the Europeans. It would be the Mutiny re-enacted.

Unrest was not confined to the blacks. Amongst the white

population war-talk was rife. Newspapers printed alarmist reports; missionaries told lurid tales of native depravity; gossip and rumour multiplied. Moreover, land-hunger affected the whites as much as the blacks. The Boers had a long standing grievance with the Zulus over the Disputed Territories, and covetous eyes began to be cast from Natal across the Tugela to the spacious rolling downs of Zululand.

Frere's eyes followed them, and it was here rather than in Natal itself that he saw the real threat to confederation and stability. It was clear to him that confederation would have to embrace Zululand, both to help relieve the pressure for new land, and to obviate the danger that the Zulu nation posed.

Relations between Natal and Cetewayo, the Zulu king, were uncertain, and complicated by a number of factors. Cetewayo had been *de facto* ruler of Zululand since 1856, when he had with the utmost ruthlessness wiped out his half-brother, Mbulazi, together with all his followers and their families – some 27,000 people in all – in an horrific massacre at a place on the Tugela known as Mathambo, 'The Place of Bones'. In 1872 Cetewayo ascended the Zulu throne by virtue of the death of his father, Mpande, and soon became embroiled with the Boers, by this time the hereditary enemies of the Zulu people, over the ownership of the Disputed Territories.

These developments had been watched with some alarm by Sir Theophilus Shepstone, the Administrator of the Transvaal, who feared that a conflict between the Zulus and the Boers might engulf Natal as well, and in order to strengthen the hand of the British in Natal, he had offered to proclaim Cetewayo heir-apparent in the name of Queen Victoria. The dubious legality of this proposal worried nobody. Mpande, Cetewayo's father, was in no position to demur, and for his part Cetewayo was vastly pleased, for he saw that the move would not only strengthen his hand in Zululand, but would also guarantee him the support of Natal should the Transvaal Boers prove aggressive, as they showed every sign of being.

When Cetewayo succeeded to the Zulu kingship at the age of forty-five, he decided to reinforce his position further by requesting Shepstone to come and officially install him as king. On 1 September 1873, in the presence of a vast concourse of

Zulus, and with great pomp and circumstance, Shepstone crowned Cetewayo king of the Zulus in the name of Queen Victoria.

There were, however, conditions attached to this mark of imperial approval, as Shepstone outlined in a long and tedious speech. The indiscriminate murders and executions, which had been a daily feature of Zulu court life for generations, were to cease. If capital punishment was necessary, it was to be preceded by a fair trial. For minor offences, confiscation of property was to be substituted for the death penalty. To all this the impatient Cetewayo was obliged to listen. None of these conditions had any binding force, as both parties knew, and Cetewayo had no intention of abiding by them. Indeed, even before Shepstone was back over the Tugela, a minor chief was caught pilfering some of the coronation presents, and in the usual fashion had his brains knocked out with a knobkerrie. John Dunn, a settler who had lived amongst the Zulus, and who was present at the coronation, thought that it served the chief right, but that the incident '. . . was the opening of the ball of killing without trial which was usual in Cetewayo's reign', and which formed one of the principal British objections to his despotic rule.

Cetewayo, then, was a barbarous despot whose land marched with that of Natal, and over whom the agencies of the Crown had a loose and ill-defined control. There were many such on the frontiers of the Empire, but what made the Zulus so alarming to Frere was their social structure and military organisation.

The original homeland of the Zulu people had been in the valley of the White Umfolozi River, but at about the time of the Napoleonic Wars, under their great and terrible King Shaka, 'the African Attila', they had expanded by a process of territorial conquest and assimilation of the tribes they had vanquished, until by the mid-nineteenth century Zululand embraced all the land and clans from the Pongola River in the north to the Tugela in the south, and from the Blood River to the Indian Ocean.

The instrument by which the Zulu nation had been created and by which it was sustained, was the army, which Shaka had forged into a terrible weapon of his will, and which Cetewayo had inherited. It was this that disturbed Frere most of all, and it was indeed a formidable organisation, unique in black Africa.

Cetewayo had at his disposal almost 50,000 warriors, or 'man destroying gladiators' as Frere put it, formed into thirty-five regiments, of whom about 40,000 could really be said to be on the active list. Although there had been no serious fighting since Cetewayo's slaughter of his rivals, all the boys of the nation were enlisted as they came of age, and went to live in military kraals in a state of enforced celibacy. The girls also were formed into regiments or guilds, though these were non-combatant. Permission to marry and to don the *isiCoco*, the head-ring which was the symbol of a married man, was seldom forth-coming until the warriors were in late middle age, and not until then were they able to settle down to a normal life.

The real strength of the Zulu armies or *impis* lay, however, not so much in their numbers, as in their discipline and organ-isation. The warriors were armed with several throwing assegais, but their principal weapon was a short broad bladed stabbing spear called the *iKlwa*,* because of the sound it made on being withdrawn from an opponent's body. They also carried a large ox-hide shield, each regiment having its own colour, both as a means of identification and to foster regimental pride. Tactics were entirely offensive, depending on hand-to-hand combat rather than on the desultory spear throwing that had always characterised Bantu warfare. An *impi* was composed of four regiments or groups of regiments. The strongest of these, usually the veterans, was known as the 'chest'; it closed as rapidly as possible with the enemy and, engaging them from the front, held them fast. Two of the other regiments, usually the younger men, formed the 'horns', and raced round the flanks of the enemy till they met, and then turned inwards, so hemming their opponents in from all sides. The remaining regiment, the 'loins', acted as a reserve, often sitting with their backs to the battle so that they should not become too excited. The whole force was controlled from some convenient emi-nence, whence the king or chief *inDuna* could send his orders

* The *iKlwa* had a blade some 1½ft long and 2in wide, mounted on a shaft about 2½ft in length.

to the regiments by runners. To all this was added the incredible mobility of the *impis*, which was underestimated by the British in 1879. The warriors, barefoot, could cover fifty miles a day. On broken ground they were a match for cavalry. They had no commissariat problems of the sort that hampered more civilised armies, and their meagre food and sleeping mats were carried by boys too young to serve in the fighting line, known as *uDibi*.

At the time of Cetewayo's accession and for some time afterwards, Zululand was at peace with its neighbours, and the great *impis* lay in idleness. But to many observers it seemed obvious that sooner or later this latent Zulu militarism would explode into active aggression. A large standing army cannot be kept inactive indefinitely, and Cetewayo's warriors were clamouring for employment. It was customary that when a new king came to the throne a campaign was organised in order that the warriors could 'wash their spears'. From this Shepstone had been able to restrain Cetewayo, but the question was whether Cetewayo could continue to restrain his regiments. 'War is the universal cry among the soldiers', wrote Shepstone, 'who are anxious to live up to their traditions.'

Against whom would this probable outburst of aggression be directed? There were three possible targets: the Swazis, the Transvaal Boers, and the British colonists in Natal. The Swazis, living to the north of Zululand, were the most probable victims. Several times Cetewayo had applied to Shepstone for permission to make 'one little swoop' to satisfy his warriors, but the Crown could not sanction a savage aggressive war, and permission was not forthcoming. The land-hungry Boers, with the Disputed Territories question always on the simmer, were certainly the next most likely target. Hatred and suspicion was mutual, even traditional, between the two races, but in April 1877 the tottering Transvaal was annexed to the Crown by Shepstone, and Cetewayo suddenly found his erstwhile enemies to be protected subjects of his friends, the British. The third possibility, that the Zulus might attack Natal, however improbable in retrospect, seemed real and alarming to Frere at the time. After Isandhlwana, Cetewayo could, had he wished, have overrun Natal, and the fact that he specifically forbade his regiments to cross the Tugela strongly suggests that he had no hostile intentions towards the British.

Frere, however, had the bit between his teeth. Cetewayo, he considered, was the root cause of the general unrest of which the Kaffir War at the Cape was but a symptom. He was by now convinced that not only confederation, but the preservation of peace in South Africa depended no longer upon the imperial or colonial authorities, '... but simply upon the caprice of an ignorant and bloodthirsty despot, with an organised force of at least forty thousand armed men at his absolute command.'* Cetewayo and the Zulu nation would have to be brought under some sort of effective British control; in particular, the *impis* would have to be disbanded. Frere realised that even if Cetewayo sincerely desired peace, he could not, with the best will in the world, demobilise his army at short notice. The whole fabric of the nation was woven round the army; its organisation directed to minister to the regiments' needs, and had been so since the time of Shaka. To disband the regiments, even if they consented to be disbanded, would create a labour surplus of 50,000 men, which the economy would be quite unable to absorb. The Zulu military machine could only be dismantled by outside agencies: and with that thought, Frere mentally resolved upon the necessity of a Zulu war.

Whatever Frere's misgivings with regard to Cetewayo's intentions towards his neighbours, they could not constitute a *casus belli*, but it was not necessary to look far to find material for one. Humanitarianism ran deep in British governments and administrators, and Zululand's internal affairs presented a spectacle to shock and outrage anyone's moral sensibilities, and in any case the Zulu king was not keeping his coronation promises.

In September 1876 there came news of a massacre ordered by Cetewayo as a result of some girls marrying without permission men of their own age, having been ordered to wed much older men. Their bodies, it was said, had been exposed in public places together with those of some of their parents who attempted to bury the corpses. On being taxed with this, Cetewayo sent a truculent message to Sir Henry Bulwer, the Governor of Natal:

* Letter to Sir Michael Hicks Beach, October 1877.

Did I ever tell Mr Shepstone I would not kill? Did he tell the white people that I made such an arrangement? Because if he did so he deceived them. I do kill; but do not consider that I have done anything yet in the way of killing. Why do the white people start at nothing? I have not yet begun; I have yet to kill; it is the custom of our nation and I shall not depart from it. Why does the Governor of Natal speak to me about my laws? Do I go to Natal and dictate to him about his laws? . . . Have I not asked the English to allow me to wash my spears since the death of my father Mpande, and they have kept playing with me all this time, treating me like a child. Go back and tell the English that I shall now act on my own account. . . . Go back and tell the white people this, and let them hear it well. The Governor of Natal and I are in like positions: he is Governor of Natal, and I am Governor here.

It was a disturbing letter.

Zululand was dotted with mission stations run by missionaries of several nations, and in May 1877 reports began to come in from them of the increasing brutality with which Cetewayo ruled. There were daily 'smellings out' of 'witches', which invariably resulted in the sudden and savage death of the offenders, who were usually unfortunates whose cattle Cetewayo wished to appropriate. It was said that, 'No sun rises or sets without its victim in Zululand.' Some of the missionaries reported that those singled out for a bloody death were often those Zulus who had been converted to Christianity, but there is some doubt as to the reliability of their testimony.

However, in June, Cetewayo again begged for permission to raid the Swazi in order to pacify the demands of his *impis*, and was again refused. Mr Bell, Commissioner for Native Affairs on the Swazi border, reported that after this Cetewayo had sent messengers to the Swazi king bidding him prepare for war against the whites. Whether or not the story contained an element of truth, it did nothing to allay Frere's fears or shake his resolve.

Frere was aware that while tales of the barbarity of Cetewayo's rule would serve to prompt the feeling in England that a war with the Zulus would minister to the cause of civilisation against a savage and bloodthirsty tyrant, he needed a more substantial excuse in order to drag a reluctant home government into yet another native war. There had been a number of border incidents between Natal and Zululand, but in July 1878 a more serious one occurred.

On the Zulu side of Rorke's Drift lived an *inDuna*, a chief named Sirayo. Two of his wives, one being his Great Wife*, Kaqwelebana, had taken lovers. While Sirayo was away at Ulundi, Kaqwelebana's eldest son, Mehlokazulu, discovered what was afoot and with three of his brothers decided to kill his mother. The deed miscarried, however, and both women and their lovers escaped across the Tugela into Natal, where they found shelter in the kraal of some native border guards. Mehlokazulu, accompanied by his uncle, crossed the river into British territory, found the younger wife, dragged her back into Zululand, where after half strangling her, they killed her with a knobkerrie. A few days later, Mehlokazulu discovered the whereabouts of his mother, and with a party of eighty followers again crossed into British territory. Kaqwelebana was hauled back across the Tugela, and shot.

This affront both to humanity and to British authority stung Bulwer into action. He reported the incident to Cetewayo and demanded that Mehlokazulu and his three brothers and their uncle should be handed over to the Natal authorities. Cetewayo replied that the two women had been guilty according to Zulu law, and that in any case the killings had not taken place in Natal. He refused to hand over the five men, and offered to pay a cattle fine instead. Bulwer saw the incident and others like it as the inevitable day-to-day friction occasioned by the presence of a barbarous native kingdom on Natal's frontier, and might have let the matter drop. Frere saw it in quite a different light, and the incident provided him with the very excuse he was looking for.

Frere was assisted in his determination to bring about a confrontation with the Zulus not only by this and other border incidents, and the tales of Cetewayo's cruelty, but also by events in London. Early in 1878, Carnarvon, disillusioned at the foundering of his hopes for confederation, resigned as secretary of state and was replaced by Sir Michael Hicks Beach. Hicks

* A Zulu could nominate any one of his several wives to be his Great Wife; her son would be his heir.

Beach lacked his predecessor's personal interest in the confederation issue, and his attitude to Frere, an elder statesman of the Empire, was almost deferential. He was inclined to trust the judgement of the man on the spot rather than his own, and his letters to Frere contain such phrases as 'I leave you, as you see, very wide discretion' and '. . . you will understand that I feel myself writing on imperfect knowledge'.* It was just what Frere, a man accustomed all his life to making large decisions, wanted. The appointment of Hicks Beach could be said to mark the point at which the government began to lose control of events in South Africa, and were pushed on to the slippery slope that led to war.

It is important to remember that the slowness of communications between London and Natal complicated the situation. The submarine cable extended only to Madeira, and a telegram from London to Cape Town took sixteen days. A letter or written dispatch took three weeks or a month, and additional time was lost while the up-country mail caught the weekly steamer to Durban and was then taken overland into the interior. A cobweb of correspondence resulted, and Hicks Beach had to labour permanently under the disadvantage of having to deal with situations weeks after they had taken place, and with information long out of date.

It was not long before Frere was sending Hicks Beach letters containing ominous phrases such as, 'It is quite clear that the war spirit is abroad . . . I have no doubt, and never have had, that the Zulus mean mischief,'† and asking for reinforcements. These were refused, but the secretary of state was rapidly losing control of the situation in Natal. In a despairing letter to the prime minister in October 1878, Hicks Beach said, 'I have sent by tonight's mail a despatch to Frere . . . throwing as much cold water as possible upon his evident expectation of a Zulu War. . . . I much fear, however, that before this can reach him we may hear of the beginning of a fight with the Zulus: and then the troops will probably have to go.' In November, also to Disraeli, Hicks Beach confessed, 'I really cannot control him [Frere] without a telegraph – (I don't know that I could

* Letters to Frere dated 25 July and 2 October 1878.
† 3 June 1878.

with one) – I feel it as likely as not that he is at war with the Zulus at the present moment. . . .'

By October, in fact, expectation of a war with the Zulus was general in London: letters of Colonial Office officials contain numerous references to it, and Hicks Beach's lack of control over Frere gave rise to some badinage. Sir William Harcourt read out in the House of Commons an imaginary letter from the secretary of state to Frere:

Dear Sir Bartle Frere. I cannot think you are right. Indeed I think you are very wrong; but after all you know a great deal better than I do. I hope you won't do what you are going to do; but if you do, I hope it will turn out well.

Hicks Beach, expressing much the same thought to Disraeli, fired off a whole series of communications to Frere telling him why a Zulu war must be avoided. The cabinet would not countenance the cost of reinforcements; the country was in financial straits; a war might involve increased taxation, which might bring down the government. Most serious of all, however, was the state of affairs in Afghanistan, and the possibility of a war there, or in Europe – with Russia. 'The fact is,' wrote Hicks Beach, 'that matters in Eastern Europe and India . . . wear so serious an aspect that we cannot now have a Zulu war in addition to other greater and too possible risks.'* Frere, however, was not prepared to shirk, or to allow the government to shirk, what he considered to be its imperial responsibilities, and replied by telegram:

I can quite see how serious is the position both in Europe and on our Indian Frontier, but I cannot think that you will mend matters by risking a greater disaster out here . . . the Zulu question is the key of everything relating to peace and war in these parts.†

To Frere, in fact, the question was no longer whether war was avoidable or inevitable, so much as the timing of its outbreak. There were a number of good reasons for precipitating the conflict. The Land-drost of Utrecht reported in October that a war

* 7 November 1878.
† Received by Hicks Beach 12 October 1878.

doctor had been visiting the Zulu military kraals, administering the charms and potions that were believed to give the warriors invulnerability; and that Cetewayo was organising large scale hunts in the area of the border where there was known to be little game. There were other reasons for taking the initiative. The Zulus' mealie harvest was not yet in, a fact that would hamper the full mobilisation of the *impis*. In January, February and March the Tugela would be high, but after that would be generally fordable, allowing Cetewayo to invade Natal – if such was his intention – at will. Later in the year, too, the grass would be dry and, by the simple expedient of burning it, the Zulus might deprive the draught animals of an invading force of grazing, thus vastly multiplying transport problems.

For all these reasons, Frere decided to bring on the crisis. On 16 November 1878, Bulwer informed Cetewayo that on 11 December a party of representative *inDunas* were to meet a British party at the Lower Tugela Drift, and here an ultimatum was delivered to the Zulus. The main points were as follows: Sirayo's three sons and their uncle were to be surrendered for trial in Natal, and fines of cattle were to be paid for their depredations and for other border incidents. A space of twenty days was to be allowed for this to be done. Other and far more significant demands were also to be met. Cetewayo was to adhere to his coronation promises regarding the casual murder of his subjects without trial; the army was to be disbanded and all the men allowed to marry; missionaries were to be allowed to carry on their activities unimpeded; a British Resident was to be received at Ulundi to make sure that these conditions were followed, and to ensure the well-being of Europeans within Zululand.

For these more important demands a period of grace of thirty days would be allowed. If they were not then met, Natal and Zululand would be at war.

Chapter two
The Invasion

The General Officer Commanding Her Majesty's troops in South Africa, Frederic Augustus Thesiger, first became cognizant of impending hostilities with the Zulus in June 1878, while still engaged upon extinguishing the Gaika and Gealeaka rising, known as the Ninth Kaffir War, in Cape Colony. It was apparent to him that a war with Cetewayo would be a far graver undertaking, and that his presence in Natal would be required to begin preparations at once. On 21 July, he wrote to the Commander-in-Chief, the Duke of Cambridge:

I leave for Natal in the *Active* on the 25th instant. Reports regarding the Zulus are very conflicting. I am quietly doing all I can to be ready for active operations against them, and Sir B. Frere is giving me every possible assistance.

Thesiger had no illusions about the nature of a war with the Zulus, or for the need for proper preparations for it. On the same day he also wrote to Sir Theophilus Shepstone:

If we are to have a fight with the Zulus, I am anxious that our arrangements should be as complete as it is possible to make them. Half measures do not answer with natives. They must be thoroughly crushed to make them believe in our superiority . . .

General Thesiger, shortly to become the second Baron Chelmsford upon the death of his father, arrived in Pietermaritzburg, the capital of Natal, on 9 August and plunged straight into the task of encompassing Cetewayo's downfall, and of defending Natal against what many believed to be the danger of imminent invasion. He was confronted with formidable difficulties.

Natal's frontier with Zululand, from the mouth of the Tugela along the river to Rorke's Drift on the Buffalo, was over 100 miles in a straight line, and very much longer along the course of the river. The frontier of the Transvaal, extending along the Blood River another hundred miles or so north-east of Rorke's Drift, also required to be defended. While a European force crossing into Zululand would be obliged to use one of the few drifts suitable for wagons, a raiding *impi*, unencumbered with heavy supplies and equipment, could cross in the opposite direction at any point along the entire frontier at any time except when the rivers were in full flood.

From Chelmsford's point of view, lateral communications along the frontier hardly existed. There was a wagon track running from the Lower Tugela Drift via Greytown to Helpmakaar, but it did so at distances from the Tugela of anything from five to twenty miles, and there was no track in the Tugela valley itself except a footpath. Even if sufficient men had been available to watch the entire frontier in strength, garrisons, wherever stationed, would be unlikely to be able to move fast enough to intercept a highly mobile *impi*. Moreover, the broken nature of the country on either side of the Tugela would not only hamper the movement of Natal's defenders, but facilitate the close and undetected approach of a Zulu force to the river.

The only answer that the Natal colonists had to this dilemma was the traditional one of the frontier: in the event of a Zulu incursion they would go into laager and stand on the defensive. Chelmsford, on purely military grounds, came rapidly to the same conclusion as Frere: that the purely passive defence of Natal was impossible. The Zulu army constituted a permanent menace, and the British must take the initiative. Sooner or later a fight was bound to occur. It had better take place in Zululand, and at a time of British choosing.

Lord Chelmsford's objects in invading Zululand were the destruction in battle of the army, the destruction of the capital, Ulundi, and if possible the capture of Cetewayo. It appeared to the general that the best way of achieving these objects would be to invade in three columns. A single strong column would certainly be able to reach and destroy Ulundi, but with their superior mobility and the fact that they could move on interior lines, Cetewayo's *impis* could always choose to avoid the blow which Chelmsford, with a complex supply problem, was anxious should be delivered quickly. Even worse, a Zulu force could simply slip behind a single British column, and raid deep into a Natal almost stripped of troops.

Chelmsford therefore resolved to send one column into Zululand from the Lower Tugela Drift, to advance on Ulundi from the south; another from Rorke's Drift, advancing eastwards; and a third to cross the Blood River and move in a south-easterly direction from the Disputed Territories. Two further columns would be kept in reserve, one covering the Middle Drift, and the approach to Pietermaritzburg, and another in the Transvaal, both of which could be called upon later as the need arose. In this way Lord Chelmsford hoped to ensure the safety of Natal and also that the main Zulu army attacked at least one of his mobile columns. It was a sound concept; the difficulty lay in the shortage of troops.

Chelmsford had six British infantry battalions available: the 2nd battalion of the 3rd Regiment (the Buffs), both battalions of the 24th, the 90th, the 1st battalion of the 13th, and the 80th. Towards the end of the year the government relented under Chelmsford's repeated requests and sent out reinforcements in the form of the 99th and 2nd/4th Regiments. Even so, when allowances had been made for the troops guarding the lines of communications and watching the approaches to Natal, the remaining imperial infantry, when divided between the three invading columns, would be precious few. Each column had to be sufficiently strong to deal if necessary with the full weight of the main Zulu army.

In order to eke out his infantry firepower – the backbone of the force – Chelmsford applied to Commodore Sullivan of the Africa Station for assistance from the navy. On 19 November a naval brigade was landed from HMS *Active* consisting of 170 sailors and marines, with two 12-pounder Armstrong guns, a Gatling and two rocket tubes, under the command of Commander Campbell, RN.

Lord Chelmsford's small army was conspicuously deficient in cavalry, and for this arm, vital against so mobile an enemy as the Zulus, he looked to the white colonists. The exigencies of frontier life had bred a proliferation of irregular, volunteer mounted units, whose splendid names, such as the Natal

Hussars, the Isipongo Mounted Rifles and the Royal Natal Carbineers, belied their uncertain training and organisation. On paper the strength of these volunteers was 660, but in fact they managed to field fewer than 300, all, however, fine horsemen and excellent shots. They were supplemented by 110 well trained and disciplined men of the regular and para-military Natal Mounted police. Had this been the sum total of the mounted men available to Chelmsford, less than 400, he would have been seriously embarrassed, but volunteers were coming in from elsewhere. Baker's Horse and the Frontier Light Horse rode up from Cape Colony. The Border Horse came down from the Transvaal, and even the Boers, setting aside their traditional hatred of the British, sent a commando forty strong. In all, the available mounted force came to about 1,000 men, enough to cover the reconnaissance needs of the three invading columns.

The only other source of manpower lay in the Natal Kaffirs. Many of them were of Zulu origin; perhaps they could be organised into a fighting force in the same way as the Indian sepoy. But here Chelmsford came up against unexpected opposition from the Lieutenant-Governor, Sir Henry Bulwer, who was deeply opposed to the creation of a trained and armed body of natives within Natal. It was not only in this matter, but in virtually every other, that the governor declined to co-operate with the general's intentions.

Bulwer was resolutely opposed to making any military preparations whatever, even the simplest ones to ensure the security of Natal, partly because he did not consider the Zulu threat serious, partly to avoid alarming the colonists and partly to avoid offering Cetewayo any provocation. He was reluctant to issue instructions to the district magistrates on the course of action to be taken in the event of a Zulu invasion; would take no steps to ensure that the police and volunteers could be mobilised and fed in the field; and wasted endless time at defence committee meetings discussing and revising the exact wording of every sentence of the orders he did issue. In short, Lord Chelmsford was hedged about by restrictions and difficulties that made his job almost impossible, and on 11 August he wrote to Frere:

I shall be truly rejoiced to welcome you as I feel my responsibilities are unduly increased by the reluctance of the Lt. Governor to allow me to take what I consider the most ordinary measures of precaution for fear lest they should be misconstrued by Cetewayo and the Zulus.

Frere hurried up to Pietermaritzburg and arrived on 28 September. Chelmsford was at last able to proceed with his arrangements, although still without Bulwer's co-operation, including the raising of the Natal Native Contingent, as it was now called.

Seven regiments of Kaffirs were raised, each 1,000 strong, and divided into two battalions, the 1st having three regiments. The NNC was, with a few notable exceptions, a dismal failure. Terrified for the most part of the Zulus, they were uncertain in attack and unreliable in defence. Although the battalion commanders and some of their subordinates were experienced British officers, the junior officers and NCOs were perforce drawn from the less desirable elements of the colony, the better men having volunteered for the mounted units. Most of them had little but contempt for their Kaffirs, and few could speak Zulu. The situation was exacerbated by the fact that the NNC lacked adequate training, for which there was no time, and by the pressing need for economy which precluded the provision of proper uniforms and equipment. The Kaffirs were obliged in the absence of a uniform to wear a red cloth around their heads to distinguish them from hostile natives, and only one man in ten was given a rifle and five rounds of ammunition, with which they proved a greater danger to their officers and NCOs than to the enemy. The rest were armed in the traditional Zulu fashion with shield, assegai and knobkerrie. Only Colonel A. W. Durnford's 1st Regiment attained anything like military proficiency, owing to that officer's zeal and his natural liking for the Kaffirs, and to the fact that he managed to obtain many of the best junior officers. He also formed three companies of the Natal Native Pioneers, and a truly loyal and efficient body of mounted Basutos known as the Natal Native Horse.

Durnford, an engineer, and soon to play a brief but controversial role in the war, had already seen active service in South Africa against the amaHlubi, during which he had lost the use of one arm. His tall figure, clad in cord breeches and serge jacket, all hung about with ammunition belts, a revolver and hunting knife, and topped with a wide-awake hat and red puggaree ('very like a stage brigand' he told his mother),* commanded the complete confidence and loyalty of his men, black and white alike. They were ready to follow him anywhere, and many of them were to fall by his side rather than desert him.

While Durnford's infantry, volunteer horsemen and native levies, with a leavening of Royal Engineers and Artillery, assembled with commendable speed, Lord Chelmsford drew up his plans in detail.

The Right Flank (or No 1) Column, which was to cross the Tugela at the Lower Drift, with Eshowe as its immediate objective, was to be commanded by Colonel Pearson of the 3rd Foot. His force comprised the 2nd/3rd Regiment, six companies of the 99th, the Naval Brigade, two 7-pounders of the Artillery, some engineers, mounted infantry and volunteers, plus the two battalions of the 2nd NNC. The total strength of his column, including the wagon crews, was 4,750, all ranks, of whom 1,852 were European combatants.

The Central (or No 3) Column, which was to cross at Rorke's Drift, and which Chelmsford himself would accompany, came under the immediate command of Colonel Glyn, 24th Foot, and was roughly of the same strength. The infantry was provided by the two battalions of the 24th. 'N' Battery, 5th Brigade Royal Artillery, provided six guns, and there were besides engineers, mounted infantry and volunteers, including the Natal Mounted Police, and the two battalions of the 3rd NNC. Of the total strength – 4,709 – 1,724 were British.

The Left Flank (No 4) Column, under the command of Colonel Evelyn Wood, VC, 90th Foot, which was to invade Zululand from the area of the upper Blood, was only about half the strength of the other combat columns, 2,278 officers and men in all, having the 90th and 1st/13th Regiments, six field guns and a cavalry force consisting of the Frontier Light Horse and Wood's Irregulars.

Durnford's native force, known as No 2 Column, was to be

* Durnford, E. *A Soldier's Life and Work* (a memoir of Col A. W. Durnford).

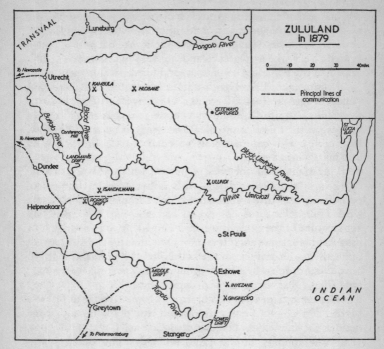

2   Zululand

kept in reserve for the defence of the border in the area of the
Middle Drift and the approaches to Pietermaritzburg, although
circumstances soon compelled its union with the Central
Column. No 5 Column, under Colonel Rowlands, VC, 1,565
strong and composed largely of the 80th Regiment and
irregular horsemen, was based on Luneburg in the Transvaal
to prevent any incursions in the north.

Lord Chelmsford's greatest problem, and one which faced
every Victorian general, was that of transport and supply.
Ulundi lay some seventy miles from the three invasion points,
but in order to reach it every round of ammunition, well over
twelve tons of it, tentage weighing nearly sixty tons, and food
at the rate of a ton a day per battalion, plus medical supplies,

cooking and engineering equipment and every other needful item, had to be moved and stock-piled in a country virtually devoid of wagon tracks, and of which no adequate maps existed. The three invading columns alone soon absorbed 5,391 oxen and other draught animals, and 756 carts and wagons.

The principal mode of transport in South Africa was the ox wagon. These, 18ft long by rather less than 6ft wide, with rear wheels as tall as a man, could carry up to 8,000lb, depending on the span of oxen, which numbered between five and nine pairs. From the *disselboom*, the shaft attached to the wagon, ran a long chain known as the *trek tow*, and to this the pairs of oxen were yoked. As well as the driver, each team required a native *voorlooper*, whose job it was to walk at the head of the leading pair. From the military point of view, the ox wagon had all kinds of disadvantages. To begin with, the oxen could not be kept in yoke for more than three or four hours at a time, or for more than eight hours a day. The remainder of the time they required to be rested and allowed to graze. Unless these conditions were met, they were inclined to die with alarming ease. The tracks, being as they were, meant that ten miles was a good day's journey. At drifts, the whole team and wagon had frequently to swim across; the Blood, for example, was 11ft deep at the time of the invasion. In particularly difficult places, wagons might have to be double-spanned or unloaded. Further, the length of a fully spanned wagon was such that on the march thirty would occupy a mile, and the impossibility of forming laager* rapidly meant that the columns would be very vulnerable if attacked while on the march. Moreover, a sufficiency of transport was difficult to obtain, since the colonists were reluctant to part with the precious teams and wagons so vital to their way of life. Inevitably, Chelmsford's officers had to buy at greatly inflated rates; a fully spanned wagon was worth £500.

Mules were also used, but although cheaper, hardier and almost as strong as oxen, they suffered from a grave drawback. Whereas in good grazing country an ox team was self-sufficient, mule teams required 120lb of fodder a day, which they had to carry in their own wagons. Thus the farther they went, the greater the proportion of their own loads they ate.

* Forming wagons into a circle, as a defensive measure.

Transport problems were to harass Chelmsford right to the end of the campaign, and he wrote to Frere in mid-September:

Transport is our greatest difficulty and the District Commissary General [Strickland] has brought it to my notice that he can neither hire or purchase it except at rates which must be considered prohibitory. I have brought our wants in this respect to the notice of the Lieut. Governor; and should a sudden emergency arise I can see no other course but to proclaim Martial Law and to impress all available private transport paying for the same at a fair and equitable rate.

The lieutenant-governor, however, resolutely opposed the introduction of martial law, and afforded Chelmsford little help with the transport problem beyond making appeals to the colonists.

Chelmsford's preparations were as thorough as they could reasonably be and, in one respect at least, his army was unusually well prepared to meet the enemy. A border agent, H. B. Fynney, whose acquaintance with the Zulus was extensive, was employed to draw up a brief profile of the Zulu army. It gave details of its strength, and of the system of recruitment, organisation and command of the regiments, the tactics of an *impi* in battle, the method by which warriors were doctored before a fight in order to give them invulnerability, and listed all the principal *inDunas*. The booklet was printed in Pietermaritzburg in November and distributed to all officers. It should have induced a feeling of respect for their enemy, but excited expectations of a swift and successful campaign were running high, and Durnford expressed an all too common sentiment when he told his mother that he expected the whole affair to be nothing more than a 'military promenade'.

Throughout December the final preparations for the invasion continued, and by the end of the year the troops were in their positions. No activity was visible in Zululand from the banks of the Tugela, and no word had been received from Cetewayo in reply to Frere's ultimatum. On 4 January 1879, therefore, the high commissioner published a final notification to the Zulu king. This rehearsed the immediate cause of Natal's quarrel with the Zulu people – the outrage committed by the sons of

Sirayo – noted that reparation had not been made, and stated that unless satisfaction had been obtained by 11 January, Lord Chelmsford was instructed to

... take such measures as the forces at his command will permit for compelling the submission of the Zulu king – always bearing in mind that the British Government has no quarrel with the Zulu nation and that the future good government and well being of the Zulus is as much an object of the steps now taken, as the safety and protection of the British territories of Natal and the Transvaal.

On the same day Wood's column, away to the north, arrived at the Blood River, and on the 6th crossed into hostile territory, where they camped to await developments. Pearson's force, at the Lower Drift, was in the event to delay its crossing until the day after the expiration of the deadline.

On 10 January, still having heard nothing from Cetewayo, Lord Chelmsford and his staff moved from Helpmakaar to join the Central Column at Rorke's Drift.

At this point the Buffalo was usually fordable, although punts had been put in place for greater convenience, and here also an old hunting trail crossed from Natal into Zululand. The continual passage of hunters and natives had broken down the banks of the river, so that a recognised crossing had been established. In 1849 a settler named James Rorke had farmed in the area, giving the place its name. The Zulus called it *kwaJimu* – 'Jim's Place'. Rorke had built a house and a barn, the latter having been turned into a chapel when a Swedish missionary named Otto Witt took the place over in 1875. Now the chapel was a store once again, and the Drift a hive of military activity. After the departure of No 3 Column, a garrison was to be left to construct a fort in order to deny the Drift to the enemy.

January 11, 1879 dawned with thick mist and rain. Chelmsford had information that Sirayo intended to dispute the crossing with 8,000 warriors. 'I hope it may be true,' he wrote to Frere. As the troops approached the river no Zulus were visible through the mist, but Lieutenant-Colonel Harness set up his six 7-pounders of 'N' Battery to cover the crossing. The horsemen splashed across into Zululand first and spread out to cover the crossing of the infantry and guns. The Natal Native Contingent crossed in the usual Zulu fashion, linking arms and dashing headlong into the neck-deep water. Several were drowned, but otherwise there were no mishaps. By mid morning the British infantry were establishing camp in Zululand, and the punts were able to start bringing the wagons over.

The ground of the Zulu side of the Buffalo rose to a ridge and then fell away to the course of a tributary stream, the Bashee. The track to Ulundi crossed this, but around the Bashee the ground was so marshy, a situation aggravated by the recent heavy rain, as to be impassable to wagons. It was evident that the column could advance no farther until the engineers and native pioneers had laid some sort of track through the marsh. The pause thus enforced upon the Central Column would be used, the general decided, to attack the kraal of Sirayo and his sons, the immediate cause of the war, which lay in a gorge beyond the Bashee.

Although the whole column turned out at 3.30 on the morning of the 12th, the attack on the kraal was to be entrusted to the 1st/3rd NNC, commanded by Colonel Hamilton-Browne, supported by four companies of the 1st/24th. The rest of the force was to remain in reserve, with the exception of the mounted men, who were to conduct a reconnaissance ahead.

Hamilton-Browne's Kaffirs had fifty Martini-Henry rifles among them, also a further fifty old muzzle-loaders which were a good deal less dangerous, since the Kaffirs, inadequately instructed, usually forgot to tear off the end of the paper cartridge, or else loaded the ball first. Hamilton-Browne was relying, somewhat optimistically, on the assegai and knobkerrie used at close quarters.

The 1st/3rd NNC advanced towards the gorge 'leaping and jumping, singing war-songs, sharpening their assegais, and looking so bloodthirsty that I feared they would kill every woman and child we came across'.* As they approached closer, however, their zeal for fighting drained away, and their advance had to be encouraged with boot and rifle-butt.

Then, at the entrance to the gorge, one of Sirayo's men called

* Hamilton-Browne, Col G. *A Lost Legionary in South Africa.*

out, asking why they were thus attacked, and Captain Dun-combe, Hamilton-Browne's interpreter, shouted back, 'By the orders of the Great White Queen.' The Zulus then seemed to retire a little, and Hamilton-Browne ordered the advance to continue; there was a splatter of shots and he ordered the charge. He was followed only by No 8 Company, composed of expatriate Zulus, with all the fighting qualities of their race. The rest of the battalion turned and fled. Behind them, how-ever, were the four 1st/24th companies, who met them with fixed bayonets, and with these at their backs, and by the liberal use of 'wild imprecations' and blows on the part of the NCOs, the Kaffirs were goaded back into the attack.

In the midst of this chaotic scene, Hamilton-Browne saw Lieutenant Harford of the 99th Regiment, who spoke fluent Zulu and who had a passion for natural history, sprawled on the ground, his sword and revolver beside him. 'Good God, Harford,' said Hamilton-Browne, 'you are hit!' 'No, sir,' replied the lieutenant, 'not hit but I have caught such a beauty,' and he proceeded to tell Hamilton-Browne the Latin name of his specimen, oblivious of the bullets falling all round. Hamilton-Browne ordered Harford back to his place at once; putting his prize in a tin, Harford obeyed and distinguished himself by capturing four of the enemy, largely owing to his ability to speak their language.

The second attack of the NNC was pressed home, and after a short skirmish Sirayo's men fled, leaving behind in the rocks twenty dead. Two men of No 8 Company had been killed, and three Europeans wounded. Sirayo's kraal was burned and 500 of his cattle taken, but the Kaffirs, mindful of Chelmsford's orders that anyone killing women, children or wounded men would be hanged, were permitted to do no further damage.

There followed a period of inactivity while a hard surface was laid through the marshy ground around the Bashee, and the track itself, now turned to mud, was improved. On the 15th, Lieutenant-Colonel Russell, 12th Lancers, commanding No 1 Squadron of the Mounted Infantry, scouted beyond the Bashee, towards Isepezi Hill, where Chelmsford intended to make his first entrenched camp and supply depot. Russell reported that there was a suitable camp site at Isandhlwana hill, ten miles away, and the general decided that this should be his immediate objective.

While waiting for the track to be made passable, Lord Chelmsford had had time to think about Durnford's No 2 Column. He now considered that better use might be made of Durnford's men, particularly the Natal Native Horse, with the Central Column. He was, besides, disturbed by the rash way in which on the 13th, having received intelligence of doubtful origin that the main Zulu *impi* was about to strike into Natal via the Middle Drift, Durnford had marched his column – entirely composed of Kaffirs except for a ten-man rocket battery – to the Tugela, prior to taking up a defensive position on the Zulu side. Had Durnford's information been accurate, his force could well have been caught between the river and the *impi*, and been annihilated. Chelmsford had only just managed to stop Durnford in time, and had sent him a rebuke beginning:

Unless you carry out the instructions I give you, it will be my unpleasant duty to remove you from your command, and to substitute another officer for the command of No 2 Column.

Chelmsford now decided to split No 2 Column, and issued the necessary instructions on the 16th. The lines of communication in Natal were already thinly defended: Durnford was therefore ordered to leave the 1st NNC in Natal – the 1st and 3rd Battalions at the Middle Drift, and the 2nd at Umsinga – and join the Central Column with the rest of his force, including three companies of the 1st/3rd NNC, on the Zulu side of Rorke's Drift. Durnford would then be under the command of Colonel Glyn and no longer able to act independently.

Durnford reached Rorke's Drift late on the 20th, to find the British camp deserted. The Central Column, having made the track passable for guns and wagons, had left for Isandhlwana that morning.

Chapter three
Isandhlwana

Isandhlwana hill, the name of which signifies 'the place like the stomach of an ox', is a narrow flat-topped eminence running north to south, some 300 yards in length, and highest at its southern end. When viewed from the side, it reminded some men of a crouching beast, and bore a curious, not to say sinister resemblance to the sphinx on the badge of the 24th Regiment. Standing just off the southern end of the hill, and connected to it by a nek,* across which ran the track from Rorke's Drift, rises a stony kopje† rather lower than Isandhlwana itself.

The terrain to the south of the hill is broken, and rises to meet the mass of Inhlazatye mountain. The horizon to the north is dominated by the escarpment of the Nqutu hills. But from the steep eastern face of Isandhlwana the ground slopes gently away in an open rectangular plain, terminated at its far end by Isepezi hill and the range of the Nkandlas. The two noteworthy features of the plain are a large donga‡ cutting across it at right-angles to Isandhlwana, and beyond this, a conical kopje rising from the level ground.

It was under the eastern face of Isandhlwana that Major C. F. Clery, Glyn's principal staff officer, proceeded to lay out the camp when the troops began to arrive at noon on 20 January. It was the best available site in the vicinity. Water was obtainable from the stream in the donga, and there was wood for fuel near at hand. Any force of enemy approaching from the direction of Ulundi, that is, from the east, would be observed out on the plain, which was devoid of cover, in ample time for the troops to assume a defensive position. It was a position from which the guns could be used with great advantage against an enemy un-

* A depression or col.
† An isolated hill.
‡ A watercourse.

provided with artillery. Although the site was not without its critics both at the time and during the controversy after the war, Lord Chelmsford himself was in no doubt as to its excellence. 'I consider,' he wrote later in a memorandum, 'that there never was a position where a small force could have made a better defensive stand.'

The camp was arranged in a line parallel with Isandhlwana. Commandant Lonsdale took his two battalions of the Natal Native Contingent to the farthest left of the camp, roughly level with the northern end of the hill. Next to him the 2nd/24th pitched their tents, with the headquarters staff and the hospital behind them, nearer the hill. Next to them again the artillery, under Colonel Harness, established themselves, with the mounted volunteer units to their right, next to the track over the nek. To the right of the track and on the extreme right of the camp, the 1st/24th camped below the stony kopje. The pioneers were arranged behind the mounted men, and behind them again spread the wagon park. Tents rapidly sprang up in a line 800 yards long, each unit dressing by its neighbour, with transport and horse lines ranged behind.

Lord Chelmsford himself rode into the new camp shortly after midday, but after a brief pause for refreshment, left to make a personal reconnaissance escorted by a few of the mounted irregulars. It was the general's intention to make quite sure that any large bodies of the enemy were swept clear of the border country before he advanced deeper into Zululand, in order to obviate the danger of a large scale raid across the Buffalo into Natal in his rear.

At the far end of the plain, beyond the conical kopje and Itelezi hill, lay the high ridge of the Nkandhla hills, and it was towards these that Chelmsford rode, with the Nqutu escarpment to his left, and opposite this, bounding the plain on its southern side, the elongated shape of Inhlazatye mountain. The general and his party rode the ten miles to the Nkandhla ridge, beyond which they could see, in the valley of the Mangeni River, the kraals of Matyana, a chief of some renown. These, however, appeared to be empty.

By about 6pm Chelmsford was back in camp. He had seen no signs of enemy activity, but was by no means satisfied that the area was in fact clear of Zulus. Wood's spies had reported that the main *impi* was to leave the royal kraal at Ulundi on 17 January. Since Ulundi was about eighty miles from Isandhlwana, Chelmsford could expect to come into contact on or shortly after the 20th. The hills around the far end of the plain could well be concealing a large number of warriors, who would doubtless use them to conceal their approach. The general therefore decided to send out a reconnaissance in strength to scout the ground at the eastern end of the plain, to commence at dawn the next morning, the 21st.

These measures were sound military common sense, but meanwhile equally important precautions were being neglected at the camp; no attempt was made to place it in a defensible state.

Before the commencement of hostilities, Chelmsford had been eager to learn from the earlier experience of the Boers, and the Regulations issued to the Field Force in November 1878 contained clear instructions regarding the laagering and entrenching of camps which the Boers had found to be a defensive measure of cardinal importance:

The camp should be formed in such a manner that the troops can be rapidly placed in a good position for action in the event of a night attack.

By night, horses should be picketed, and oxen placed in wagon laager, the camp guarded by outlying pickets of infantry thrown out at short distances to the front, flanks and rear, with small parties of natives – ten men in each – interspersed and placed in situations where they could give timely warning of the approach of an enemy.

The camp should be partially entrenched on all sides.

The absolute importance of laagering the wagons and putting each camp into a defensible state had been impressed upon Chelmsford by no less a person than Paul Kruger and, on the same day that Isandhlwana was reached, the general had received a visit from J. J. Uys, a redoubtable old Zulu-fighter, who told him: 'Be on your guard and careful . . . Trek into Zululand with two laagers close to each other. Place your spies far out, and form your wagons into a round laager. The Zulus are more dangerous than you think.' In reply to this advice,

'The General smiled, and said that he thought it was not necessary.'*

After the Isandhlwana disaster, a fierce debate sprang up as to why the camp had not been laagered. For his part, Lord Chelmsford was clear '. . . that as regards outposts patrolling and ordinary protection of the camp . . . Colonel Glyn was solely responsible.'† But this will not do: so vital a decision could not have been left to the column commander, and if Glyn had failed to laager, then Chelmsford should have rectified the omission when he returned from his reconnaissance across the plain. To do so, after all, would only have been to obey his own instructions as laid down in the Regulations.

In fact, the evidence suggests that Colonel Glyn *did* suggest laagering, but that Chelmsford overruled him. According to Colonel E. Durnford he did so scornfully, with the words, 'It would take a week to make.'

It is undeniably true that the forming of a laager would have been an enormous task, time consuming and exhausting for men and oxen alike: an ox wagon was not a readily manoeuvrable vehicle. And any laager could only have been a temporary affair, since many of the wagons were needed to return to Rorke's Drift. The task of entrenching would also have been costly in effort and time. There were only a few native pioneers available, the ground was hard and stony, and the camp site was 800 yards long. To Chelmsford, who had as yet no concept of how swiftly a Zulu *impi* could move, or the ease with which it could conceal itself, the most pressing need was to push on to Cetewayo's capital as rapidly as possible. If he paused to make every camping place impregnable, it would take him longer to reach Ulundi than he could afford. Besides, the pickets and the outlying vedettes would give adequate warning of an attack, and nobody on the staff at least was in any doubt as to the outcome of a set-piece fight in the open if the Zulus fell upon a British square supported by artillery. Indeed, it was just such a battle that Chelmsford sought, and the action at Ulundi later vindicated his confidence in this respect.

* Durnford, E. *A Soldier's Life and Work.*
† Atkinson, C. T. *The South Wales Borderers.*

Nevertheless, the failure to take precautionary defensive measures at the camp caused much disquiet amongst many of the officers, both colonial and imperial, however complacent the staff.

Commandant Lonsdale joined Hamilton-Browne (known as 'Maori' Browne from his fighting experience in New Zealand), and his first words were, 'My God, Maori, what do you think of this camp?' 'Someone is mad,' replied Hamilton-Browne. Another colonial officer, Duncombe, said, 'Do the staff think we are going to meet an army of schoolgirls? Why in the name of all that is holy do we not laager?' Hamilton-Browne took it upon himself to mention the matter to Glyn, who had served under Browne's father. Glyn 'did not seem to be in good spirits, but said nothing about the camp and on my remarking it looked very pretty though rather extended, he looked hard at me, shook his head and said "very" '.*

Lieutenant Melvill, adjutant of the 1st/24th, discussed the defensive arrangement with an officer of the 2nd Battalion and said: 'I know what you are thinking by your face, sir: you are abusing this camp and you are quite right. These Zulus will charge home and with our small numbers we ought to be in laager. . . .'

The lack of proper defensive arrangement would not have been quite so bad had the pickets and vedettes been posted more thoroughly. No look-out was established on the top of Isandhlwana itself, and no pickets were posted to the west of the hill. In other words, the rear of the camp was quite un-provided for. A staff officer told Mr Mansel of the Natal Mounted Police that 'the rear always protects itself!' Mansel was not at all happy with the situation. He had been ordered to post the cavalry vedettes, and having done so, was told by the staff officer that those up on the Nqutu escarpment were 'far too far away and were of no use there'.† Mansel was ordered to draw his vedettes in, and rode off on what he considered to be a fool's errand.

When Mansel reached his men on the Nqutu, a Zulu was seen running off in the distance. He was chased and caught, and

* Hamilton-Browne, Col G. *A Lost Legionary in South Africa.*
† Durnford, E. *A Soldier's Life and Work.*

told Lieutenant Phillips, Mansel's subaltern, who spoke Zulu, 'Why are you looking for the Zulus this way? The big *impi* is coming from that direction,' and the old man pointed across the Nqutu range. Mansel sent Phillips into the camp to report this information. Lord Chelmsford, who was at dinner, said that it was of no importance, but that the Zulu should present himself next day, which needless to say he did not do.

The evening of the 20th passed off quietly enough. Norris-Newman, the *Standard* newspaper correspondent, recorded that 'our mess had a jolly little dinner'. Those who had been detailed for the reconnaissance on the morrow were in high spirits, and those who were not bemoaned their bad luck. For most of them, it was to be worse than anything they could have imagined.

The reconnaissance in strength was to be in two parts. Major Dartnell was to take 150 of the mounted men from the Natal Mounted Police, the Natal Carbineers, the Newcastle Mounted Rifles and the Buffalo Border Guard. The men were to carry a day's rations and were to scout thoroughly the far end of the plain, Isepezi hill, the Nkandhlas and beyond them Matyana's kraals in the Mangeni valley. Commandant Lonsdale was ordered to take the two battalions of the 3rd Natal Native Contingent behind Inhlazatye mountain and work his way towards the Mangeni River until he met Dartnell. In this way, Chelmsford considered that if the *impi* had approached to a position behind the hills from the direction of Ulundi, it would not remain undetected. Major Dartnell's force was to be accompanied by Major Gosset and Captain E. H. Buller (not to be confused with Redvers Buller, referred to later), two of the general's ADCs.

Lonsdale's force left the camp before first light on the 21st, but the country to the south of Inhlazatye was rough and over-grown with thorn bushes, and the going was heavy. Lonsdale split his force, sending the 2nd Battalion under Cooper along the top of the hills, while Hamilton-Browne moved up the valley below with the 1st Battalion searching the kraals, which were for the most part deserted. His men did, however, find two Zulus who had deserted from the army at Ulundi, and who confirmed the suspicion entertained by Chelmsford that the *impi* would be in the Isandhlwana area in the very near future.

Late in the afternoon, Lonsdale debouched from the hills seven miles from the camp, and three miles away from Dartnell's mounted men, who were visible on the Nkandhlas ridge. His force was exhausted from scrambling about in the thorn-covered hills, and very hungry; the NNC had not eaten for twenty-eight hours. He therefore sent a party back towards Isandhlwana with some livestock he had captured, and directed Lieutenant Harford to ride ahead to see what Dartnell intended to do. Harford was back again within the hour with important news.

Dartnell, like Lonsdale, had split his force, sending some of his men up to the northern end of Inhlazatye mountain near where Lonsdale was to emerge, and leading the rest across the Mangeni. There, where the plain rose towards the eastern end of the Nqutu, he had come across large numbers of Zulus, possibly the vanguard of the main *impi*. He had sent Gosset and Buller back to Lord Chelmsford with a request for reinforce-ments and permission to attack in the morning. Dartnell intended spending the night where he was on the hills, and he asked Lonsdale to join him. Lonsdale concurred in this plan, for he was spoiling for a fight, but at least one of his officers, Hamilton-Browne, protested strongly against the idea. As he pointed out, the Kaffirs of the NNC had had no food since noon the day before, nobody had any blankets, and there was little ammunition between them, since a battle had not been expected. The natives were unreliable at the best of times; they would certainly not face the Zulus when cold, hungry, sleepless and ill-armed. Lonsdale, however, would not listen, and marched his exhausted and unwilling natives to join Dartnell. Several European officers and NCOs, privately agreeing with Hamilton-Browne, seized their opportunity to slip away unobserved and return to the main camp, little knowing what the price of their desertion would be.

Chelmsford had not rested content with sending out Dartnell and Lonsdale to scout towards the end of the plain, and had himself spent a busy day trying to anticipate the moves the *impi* would make as it approached the Central Column. It was certain that the Zulu army must by now have covered most of the distance between Ulundi and Isandhlwana. It was probable that for the greater part of the distance they would keep to the track, leaving it somewhere in the vicinity of Isepezi hill, since they would have no wish to attack across several miles of open plain. On reaching Isepezi, therefore, the *impi* would either turn south and approach the camp behind Inhlazatye, or swing north, and advance hidden by the Nqutu plateau. In either case, it would be able to get within a couple of miles of the camp unseen, unless detected by scouts. Chelmsford considered that if the *impi* swung southwards, Dartnell and Lonsdale would find it; so the danger zone seemed to be the Nqutu escarpment and plateau. After despatching a party of mounted infantry under Lieutenant Brown to scout Isepezi again, the general decided to conduct another personal reconnaissance, this time on the Nqutu escarpment.

Accompanied by a few of his staff and a small escort, Chelmsford rode up to the vedettes, the farthest away of which was some two miles along the ridge, roughly opposite the conical kopje on the plain. Reaching the vedette at 3pm, Chelmsford discovered that despite the excellent view, the men, like their comrades nearer the camp, had seen no sign of enemy movement. Then, just as the general was leaving, fourteen mounted Zulus rode over a ridge a mile off, halted, and seeing the British party, departed as suddenly as they had appeared.

It was on the way back to the camp that Buller and Gosset caught up with Chelmsford, and delivered Dartnell's message. The general was displeased. Dartnell had been sent out on a reconnaissance, and not to fight a battle. Wherever the *impi* was, the Zulus in front of Dartnell, those seen by Brown (who had returned from Isepezi having exchanged shots with another party of warriors), and the group seen by Chelmsford himself, all indicated that the Zulu army was drawing near. Chelmsford had no wish for his force to be divided, and considered that Dartnell had exceeded his orders. It was, however, too late in the afternoon to get Dartnell and Lonsdale back to Isandhlwana before dark, so while refusing the requested reinforcements the general sent some pack horses loaded with blankets and food, with a mounted infantry escort, plus permission to attack in the morning, at Dartnell's discretion.

Dartnell, meanwhile, had discovered that the situation was not developing in quite the way he had expected, for as the light began to fade, more and more Zulus were observed joining the force facing him. He estimated that they now numbered in excess of 1,500 – perhaps as many as 2,000. When Inspector Mansel took a mounted scouting party to probe the Zulu position, they at once assumed their classic offensive formation, and sent two horns dashing round the flanks of the horsemen, who beat a hasty retreat. It began to look as though Dartnell had found part of the main *impi*. There were certainly too many Zulus for him to handle, so he sent a second messenger back to Lord Chelmsford, this time asking for two or three of the British infantry companies.

The mounted men then formed square and settled down for an uncomfortable night, for the blankets and food sent out to them from the camp were insufficient to go round. Lonsdale's two NNC battalions formed a square nearby, with the white officers and NCOs in the centre. 'Maori' Browne, whose disgust with the fighting qualities of the Natal Kaffirs knew no limits, decided to disarm the natives and give their rifles and ammunition to the whites, few of whom had their weapons with them. Hamilton-Browne then loosened his revolver belt, and grasping his horse's bridle firmly, lay down and went to sleep.

He was suddenly awakened as a mass of natives trampled over him, and on trying to scramble to his feet, was promptly knocked down again. It looked as if the Zulus had fallen on the sleeping square: the Kaffirs were rushing around, shouting and panicstricken, while the horses of the Europeans plunged about in the dark causing more confusion and not a little danger. 'My God,' thought Hamilton-Browne, 'why am I not assegaied?' But it was, luckily, a false alarm, and upon seeing this he grabbed a knobkerrie from the nearest Kaffir and started laying about him. 'My white men fought their way to my shout and backing me up splendidly we soon quelled the uproar and thrashed the cowardly brutes back to their places.' Dartnell's men had stood firm during this commotion, unable to see what was happening and not knowing what to expect. Before the night was out, they were to be aroused by a second disturbance in the NNC square, again occasioned by a false alarm.

Darkness had overtaken Dartnell's second messenger out on the plain. As it was a moonless night, he was slowed to a foot-pace, and it was not until half-past one in the morning of the 22nd that he reached the camp, to find the general asleep.

To Chelmsford, the implication of the message was clear. He was sure that the *impi* was not on the Nqutu plateau, which he had inspected himself on the previous afternoon. He felt equally certain that it could not have slipped behind Inhlazatye without Lonsdale's force having seen it. It looked, therefore, as if Dartnell had run into the main *impi*, or part of it at least, since the only Zulus thought to be in the area of the eastern end of the plain, Matyana's people, were certainly not so numerous as the force Dartnell was reporting to his front.

Dartnell, in his eagerness to get into action, had by his decision to spend the night out on the hills, rather than return to the camp, thus unwittingly placed Lord Chelmsford in a cleft stick. If it was indeed the main *impi* that Dartnell had contacted, the 2,000 or so warriors he had seen would be but the tip of the iceberg; the *impi* was known to be at least 20,000 strong, perhaps more. The troops under Dartnell and Lonsdale – 150 mounted men and 1,400 Kaffirs – if caught by such a force would be savagely mauled, even destroyed, if unable to retire at first light. The need to reinforce Dartnell was therefore urgent, but compelled Chelmsford to do the very thing he wished to avoid: to split his column at the moment when a battle seemed imminent. It had nevertheless to be done, and quickly.

It appeared to Chelmsford that if the *impi* was at the end of the plain, it was there, rather than at the camp, that battle, if battle were offered, would take place; he therefore decided to accompany the force going to Dartnell's relief himself. It was, however, vital to ensure that both the reinforcement and the force left to guard the camp should be sufficiently strong to deal with the *impi* if the need arose.

The imperial infantry with the Central Column consisted of five companies of the 1st Battalion of the 24th Regiment – two more were at Helpmakaar and one in Natal – and seven companies of the 2nd Battalion of the 24th, one other, 'B' Company, being at Rorke's Drift. Chelmsford decided to split the infantry equally; to take six companies of the 2nd/24th with him, and leave the 1st/24th, plus Lieutenant Pope's 'C' Company, 2nd/24th, which was on outpost duty, in the camp.

The Central Column's six guns were provided by Lieut-Colonel Harness, with 'N' Battery, Royal Artillery; of these, the general decided to take Harness with four, and leave Lieutenant Curling with the other two. Major Stuart Smith, Harness's second in command, elected to go along for the ride. Since the plain was known to be seamed with dongas, the native pioneers would accompany the artillery in order to facilitate the passage of the guns. The force going out to find Dartnell was completed by the addition of some mounted infantry under Lieut-Colonel Russell. The force, like the Central Column itself, was to be under the immediate command of Colonel Glyn, with Chelmsford and his staff accompanying.

The troops remaining in the camp were to be left under the command of Colonel Pulleine, and numbered, including various odd details, about 1,200 men, of whom more than 800 were Europeans. In addition to the six companies of the 1st and 2nd/24th, and the artillerymen, numbering seventy-two of all ranks, there were thirty-three Natal Mounted Policemen, fifty-five mounted irregulars, thirty mounted infantry, eleven Natal Native Pioneers, and four companies of the Natal Native Contingent.

Reveille rang out at about 2am, and while the troops were getting under arms, Chelmsford summoned Glyn and Lieut-Colonel J. N. Crealock, his military secretary, to issue two important orders. These, in the light of events, were of the greatest significance.

One was to Pulleine, investing him with the command of the camp. The instructions contained in it were clear. He was to keep his troops within the camp, acting upon the defensive; to draw in the infantry pickets; and to keep the screen of cavalry patrols far out. These orders, transmitted via Glyn, were delivered to Pulleine in writing, and Major C. F. Clery, Glyn's staff officer, went to Pulleine's tent and repeated them verbally.

The other order, despatched this time by Crealock, was to Colonel Durnford down at Rorke's Drift. The troops with Durnford consisted of 300 mounted natives, composed of Sikali's Horse under Lieutenant Henderson, and Newnham-

Davis with the Edendale contingent. There were also three companies of the 1st/3rd NNC, 'D' Company under Captain Nourse and 'C' Company under Captain Stafford, and Major Francis Russell's rocket battery. It occurred to Chelmsford that Durnford could reach Isandhlwana in time to reinforce the camp should a battle develop later in the day.

The precise text of the order to Durnford is important, for it does *not* contain, as the *Official Narrative* states, a directive to him to assume command of the camp when he arrived. The version of these instructions given in the *Official Narrative* is as follows:

Before leaving, Lord Chelmsford sent orders to Colonel Durnford, RE, who was at Rorke's Drift, to advance at once to Isandhlwana with all his mounted men and the rocket battery, and *as senior officer to take command of the camp*.* This, till his arrival, was left in charge of Lieutenant-Colonel Pulleine, 2/24th Regiment.

The actual order sent to Durnford – who copied it into his notebook, later found on the field of Isandhlwana – ran thus:

22nd, Wednesday, 2 am.
You are to march to this camp *at once* with all the force you have with you of No 2 Column.
Major Bengough's battalion is to move to Rorke's Drift as ordered yesterday.
2/24 Artillery and mounted men with the General and Colonel Glyn move off at once to attack a Zulu force about ten miles distant.

J.N.C.

P.S. If Bengough's battalion has crossed the river at Eland's Kraal it is to move up here (Nangwani Valley).

A number of the wagons were due to return next day to Rorke's Drift, but in order not to weaken the camp unnecessarily by the provision of an escort for them, and to avoid the danger of their being caught in the open should a fight develop, Chelmsford cancelled the movement, and the message to Durnford was given to Lieutenant† Horace Smith-Dorrien of the 95th Regiment, who was employed on transport duties, to deliver.

* Author's italics.
† Later, General Sir.

Smith-Dorrien rode off over the nek in the direction of Rorke's Drift, and shortly afterwards, at about 3.30am, Glyn's force marched out to the relief of Dartnell.

Lord Chelmsford and his staff rode on ahead of the column, and reached Dartnell and Lonsdale and their sleepless men at 6am, only to find that the hills ahead were now devoid of Zulus. The *impi*, if such it had been, had vanished with the darkness, leaving only a few individuals making their belated way over the ridge.

The general resolved to scour the area to the north at once, and try to locate the Zulu army. Lonsdale's two native battalions were directed to advance along the ridge, and Dartnell took the mounted men around its southern side. Word was sent back to Glyn, whose progress across the plain had been slow, to take his troops to the north of the ridge. The principal cause of Glyn's delay was the difficulty of dragging the guns over the dongas which cut across the plain. Detaching two of the infantry companies to escort the artillery, Glyn pushed on as fast as possible with the remainder. He was, however, too late to participate in the skirmish which developed on the ridge. As the Natal Native Contingent advanced, they flushed out a number of Zulus who had been hiding amongst the rocks. Some of these took refuge in caves, where they were trapped and killed, but the rest were driven off the ridge and caught by the mounted men, who killed about thirty of them. Glyn's infantry arrived in time to help see the last few Zulus off, by which time it was 9.30, and Chelmsford ordered a halt for breakfast.

The whereabouts of the main *impi*, assuming that it had arrived in the area from Ulundi, was still unknown; all Chelmsford could be certain of was that it was not in the vicinity of the eastern end of the plain. He now decided, without spending more time in looking for the enemy, to establish the next camp in the Mangeni valley, and sent Major Stuart Smith and Captain Alan Gardiner back to Pulleine with an order to strike camp at Isandhlwana and join him. Crealock sent for 'Maori' Browne and ordered him to take his battalion of Natal Kaffirs back to the camp to assist Pulleine to move, and to ensure at the same time that the line of communication with Isandhlwana was clear. Crealock was enjoying his breakfast and Hamilton-

Browne, though very hungry, declined to join him, as his men were still without food. Hamilton-Browne, a veteran of colonial warfare, was by no means as satisfied as Chelmsford and his staff that the area was in reality as clear of Zulus as it appeared, and inquired what he should do if, with his faint-hearted Kaffirs, he should become engaged. ' "Oh!" said he [Crealock], "just brush them aside and go on," and with this he went on with his breakfast.'

It was now about 10am, and as Hamilton-Browne set off, a horseman arrived with a message to Lord Chelmsford from Pulleine: 'Staff Officer – Report just come in that the Zulus are advancing in force from left front of camp. 8.5am.' This laconic communication contained no hint of an emergency, and Chelmsford was not disturbed by it. He had left a force in the camp strong enough to defend it against all comers, and it would in any case be impossible to get Glyn's troops back to Isandhlwana until some five hours after Pulleine's message had been despatched. If the thought occurred to Chelmsford that the main *impi* had moved into a position on the Nqutu plateau from which it could menace the camp he did not express the idea to his staff. To satisfy himself, however, the general sent Lieutenant B. Milne, his naval ADC, representing the Naval Brigade, to the top of a near-by hill, from where Isandhlwana was visible. Climbing into a tree, Milne focused his powerful naval telescope on the distant camp. The tents were still standing and there were no signs of any abnormal activity. Chelmsford was reassured and determined to push on to the new camping ground, there to await the arrival of the rest of the Central Column from Isandhlwana.

It was not long before the units with Chelmsford were widely separated in their advance. Russell and the mounted infantry were combing the ground to the north. Harness's four guns and their escort of the 2nd/24th under Captain Church were making their way independently, as was the general himself, who was riding ahead with Glyn to select the precise spot for the new camp. At about noon, Lonsdale informed Major Gosset, one of Chelmsford's aides, that he was returning to Isandhlwana in order to obtain food for his two NNC battalions, who were by this time in a bad way.

At 12.15 two prisoners taken by the mounted infantry were brought in and interrogated by Longcast, the interpreter. They said that the main *impi* from Ulundi was due to arrive at Isandhlwana that day, and then, catching the sound of distant gunfire, they exclaimed, 'Do you hear that? There is fighting going on at the camp!'

Chelmsford and his staff at once galloped up the nearest rise, from where, through field-glasses, they could see the camp at Isandhlwana. The tents were still standing, as Milne had reported earlier, and figures could be seen moving to and fro between them. As they watched, shells could be seen bursting on the Nqutu escarpment. There was undoubtedly some kind of a fight in progress at the camp, but Chelmsford still saw no reason to be disturbed. He was satisfied that the force left in the camp, which should by now have been reinforced by Durnford, could beat off any attack launched against it, and when the firing died away he assumed that this was what had happened.

Harness and Church had also seen the bursting shells and were puzzled as to how best to act. Then, about 1pm, having decided to press on to the new camp-site, they saw some five miles away, between them and Isandhlwana, a large body of natives. This, they presumed, was Hamilton-Browne's battalion returning to the camp, but as they watched, a mounted man left the column and came towards them at a gallop. Harness halted the guns and sent Church to meet the rider half-way. Within a quarter of an hour, Church was back with a message from Hamilton-Browne as horrifying as it was brief: 'For God's sake come back with all your men; the camp is surrounded and must be taken unless helped.'

Harness had been joined by Gosset, who, though uneasy, did not believe the report. But Harness immediately said, 'I presume under the circumstances I had better move towards the camp' (i.e. Isandhlwana). Gosset was doubtful and suggested that one of Harness's officers should return with him to the general for definite orders. This was done, but Harness in the meanwhile set off at once, only to be overtaken a mile on by Gosset, who ordered him to turn the guns about once more and proceed to the new camp-site. It is by no means clear that Gosset delivered

Hamilton-Browne's message to Chelmsford; if he did, it must have been in a watered down version, for even at this stage, the general's confidence in Pulleine's ability to defend the camp was not to be shaken. At about 2pm, however, he did decide to ride back towards Isandhlwana to see for himself what was happening, but did so at a rather leisurely pace, for the horses were by this time tired. Russell's mounted infantry accompanied the general as escort, leaving the troops under Dartnell, Harness and Glyn to push on to the new camp-site.

'Maori' Browne had in fact despatched three messages to Lord Chelmsford, the one which reached Gosset and Harness being the last. While still some eight miles from Isandhlwana Hamilton-Browne and one of his officers, Lieutenant Campbell, saw two Zulus and rode after them. Campbell shot one, but Hamilton-Browne rode the other one down and captured him. On questioning the man, they learned that he had been detached from the main *impi*, which he said was on the Nqutu plateau, to scout the far end of the plain. The *impi* was twelve regiments strong – 20,000 men at least. Hamilton-Browne wrote a note containing this intelligence and sent it to Chelmsford by Lieutenant Pohl.

He then rode on a mile or two ahead of his battalion, and met two Kaffirs carrying some rations, two bottles of whisky and a note from two lieutenants of the 1st/24th, saying that they had visited his tent on the previous evening and had eaten the dinner Hamilton-Browne's cooks had prepared for him; the whisky was by way of repayment. After receiving this bizarre communication, Hamilton-Browne rode back to his natives and distributed the food, which unfortunately did not go very far.

His battalion then advanced another mile, to a place from which Hamilton-Browne could see the shells bursting against the Nqutu escarpment. Not knowing that Chelmsford was able to see this for himself, Hamilton-Browne sent Sergeant Turner off with a message to this effect. At about this time Lieutenant Pohl returned. He had been unable to find Chelmsford, but had given the message he carried to Colonel Russell to deliver to the general. By some coincidence, Turner also ran across Russell, and gave the colonel *his* message to pass on. Chelmsford, therefore, must have received Hamilton-Browne's first two messages, or the gist of them, simultaneously. It may be that in the process they lost some of their original force and sense of urgency.

From where Hamilton-Browne and his Natal Kaffirs stood, large numbers of Zulus were now visible. Again Hamilton-Browne rode forward ahead of his men, to gain a better view, and this time approached to within four miles of the camp. He could see hordes of Zulus advancing over the edge of the Nqutu escarpment and pouring down on to the plain, where they were spread out in a huge crecsent-shaped line which over-lapped both flanks of the camp. Hamilton-Browne was in no doubt as to what it was he saw or of the gravity of the situation. He galloped back to his battalion, formed them into a defensive ring, with the Europeans in the middle, and sent Captain Develin racing back to find Chelmsford with his third, desperate, message – the one which reached Harness and Gosset.

Hamilton-Browne's NNC battalion would go no farther. They had been without food for two days, on both of which they had been subjected to strenuous exertions. After a sleepless night, they had already been involved in one skirmish with a body of Zulus, whom they dreaded. Ahead there lay, apparently, Zulus in vast and overwhelming numbers. It was too much. Hamilton-Browne decided under the circumstances to stay put for a while and await developments.

As Chelmsford and the mounted infantry rode slowly in the direction of Isandhlwana, a second message from Pulleine arrived. It was as brief and as cool as the first had been: 'Staff Officer. Heavy firing to the left of our camp. Cannot move camp at present.'

Again, there was nothing to suggest any sort of an emergency at the camp. Shortly after this, a third messenger rode in from Isandhlwana, with a note addressed to Major Clery: 'Heavy firing near left of camp. Shepstone has come in for reinforcements and reports that Zulus are falling back. The whole force at camp turned out and fighting about one mile to left flank.'

Clery already knew that a fight of some kind was taking place at the camp, and the reference to Captain George Shepstone, Durnford's Political Assistant, indicated that Durnford's troops had arrived. He therefore considered that the note contained nothing of any significance and did not bother to show it to Lord Chelmsford.

Sometime after 3pm the general and his staff and escort came upon Hamilton-Browne and his demoralised Kaffirs, still awaiting events. Chelmsford would not believe Hamilton-Browne's story that the camp had fallen, or that their way back to the camp might be blocked; ordering the 1st/3rd NNC to fall in behind the mounted infantry, he rode on.

At 3.30, and still five miles from Isandhlwana, Chelmsford saw a solitary figure riding towards him on an exhausted horse. It was Commandant Lonsdale and he bore terrible tidings to the incredulous general.

The camp at Isandhlwana was in the hands of the Zulus and there was not a British soldier left alive.

Lonsdale, it will be remembered, had ridden back to the camp to ensure that his Kaffirs received the supplies they so badly needed. He was exhausted and hungry after the exertions of the past two days, and after a sleepless night; he was also feeling unwell. He rode along without paying much attention, half asleep in his saddle. Dot, his pony, was as tired as he. As he approached the tents at about 2pm, a native fired at him, but even this failed to bring Lonsdale entirely to his senses. He thought it was a careless Kaffir: they were notoriously dangerous with guns. Then, as he rode up to the tents, the frightful truth rushed in upon him. There were no white soldiers to be seen. The men wearing the red British jackets were *Zulus*. One of them appeared from within a tent, a bloodied assegai in his hand. They were everywhere, amongst the tents and wagons, busy upon an orgy of looting and destruction. Lying thick on the ground, in every direction, were the dead and mutilated bodies of the British soldiers and Natal Kaffirs. It was a scene of unimaginable chaos and slaughter.

Lonsdale turned his pony and, applying whip and spur, just managed to goad the exhausted beast into a trot, while assegais and bullets tore about him. Had the Zulus not been so busy looting, it is certain that he would have been killed immediately. After a few hundred yards, Dot collapsed; Lonsdale had to pull her to her feet and drag her along. It took him nearly two hours to cover the five miles that separated him from Chelmsford.

The general was stunned, recalled Norris-Newman, the *Standard* correspondent. There was now no element of doubt; yet the truth was for a moment too horrifying, too overwhelming to grasp.

'I can't understand it,' said Lord Chelmsford. 'I left a thousand men there.'

The principal cause of the disaster at Isandhlwana which now confronted Chelmsford so starkly was simply lack of information. Wood's spies had reported, quite correctly, that the main *impi* had been sent from Ulundi towards the Central Column on 17 January. From this information, the general had surmised, also quite correctly, that it must have reached the area of Isepezi and Isandhlwana by the 20th. But here Chelmsford's intelligence system broke down; and here it was that the Zulus had the advantage of him.

Cetewayo knew that the British were invading his kingdom in three columns, and had despatched two smaller forces to confront the right and left flanking columns, while throwing his main strength against the Central Column. He gave no specific instructions to his *inDunas*, beyond the fact that they were to destroy the invaders, or drive them back into Natal.

The Zulus had no concept of a defensive strategy. They could try to surround the British, whom they outnumbered heavily, and they could cut the columns' communications with Natal. When a suitable opportunity presented itself, they would employ their traditional tactics of hurling every available warrior forward, with the encircling horns crushing the enemy in their deadly embrace against the chest.

As the Central Column and the *impi* approached one another, the Zulus held all the trump cards. The British, with their guns and wagons, were slow and cumbersome; the Zulus were swift and highly mobile. The British were conspicuous; the Zulus were past masters at concealing large bodies of warriors in long grass or on broken ground. Finally their spies were everywhere, swiftly and silently moving over the land to observe every move the British made.

On the night of 20/21 January, the *impi* had bivouacked off the Ulundi track, to the north-west of Isepezi hill, about eight miles from the tribal force found by Dartnell, and fifteen miles from the camp at Isandhlwana. Although Chelmsford had not seen the *impi*, his suspicion that it was in the Isepezi area was therefore quite correct. The Zulus, better informed than the British general, knew that a force (Dartnell's) had left the camp and advanced to the eastern end of the plain. and that the strength of the troops in the camp was thereby reduced. During the day of 21 January, the *impi* moved stealthily, undetected by the vedettes on the Nqutu escarpment, to a position in a rocky valley on the north-east side of the plateau, about five miles from Isandhlwana. Here, in silence and without lighting fires, the Zulu army spent the night of the 21st/22nd.

Chelmsford, meanwhile, had further split his force by going to Dartnell's assistance in the early hours of the 22nd. Of this also the Zulus were informed, and must undoubtedly have wondered at their good fortune. The British were putting themselves into a position to be destroyed piecemeal. As an *inDuna* said afterwards, 'You gave us the battle by splitting up into small parties.'

The Zulus did not, however, intend to attack on the 22nd, which was the day of the new moon, and therefore 'dark' and unpropitious. They proposed to wait concealed in their valley for twenty-four hours, and fall upon the British camp on the 23rd. But for them, as for the British, events did not work out quite as expected.

After Lord Chelmsford and Colonel Glyn had left the camp to go to the relief of Dartnell, Pulleine set about arranging his outposts for the day. Two companies of the NNC were posted to the left of the camp, and another on the spur leading up to the Nqutu escarpment. Beyond them a small vedette was posted, though the one farther along the edge of the plateau, opposite the conical kopje, which Mansel had been ordered to withdraw on the previous day, was not re-established. In front of the camp, out towards the big donga, 'G' Company of the 2nd/24th under Lieutenant Pope and his second-in-command, Lieutenant Godwin-Austen, was strung out on a 1,000-yard front.

At 7.30am the bugles sounded the call to breakfast and men fell in at the field kitchens behind the tent lines. At about eight o'clock, however, before the men could finish their meal, a rider from the vedette on the escarpment came galloping in with the news that a large number of Zulus had been seen advancing across the plateau. The fall-in sounded; struggling into their belts and straps, the men seized their rifles and fell in line in front of the tents. Pope's company, and the two NNC companies, fell back to the camp. The quartermasters stood to the ammunition wagons, while the bandsmen of the 1st/24th assembled behind the tents; their duty was to act as stretcher bearers. Pulleine despatched his first message to Lord Chelmsford.

Nothing more was heard from the vedette, nor were any Zulus seen. Then, after about an hour, a few warriors were observed several miles away on the rim of the plateau, and a second messenger galloped up to say that the Zulus had been in three groups. One had moved off to the north-west and the other two had disappeared to the north-east. There appeared to be no immediate threat to the camp, so the men were put at ease, but still in their positions.

They were still under arms when, at 10am, Colonel Durnford rode over the nek and into the camp, with his force behind him, and went to look for Pulleine. Pulleine explained the situation: that the general had gone to extricate Dartnell and Lonsdale; that two messages had been received saying that Zulus had been seen moving up on the plateau; and that his orders were to act on the defensive. At the court of inquiry which sat after the disaster, Lieutenant Cochrane, a member of Durnford's staff, who was present at the interview, said that Pulleine repeated the order to defend the camp several times.

Durnford was four years senior to Pulleine and the command of the camp automatically became his responsibility, although Crealock's order had not actually mentioned this. After the event there was some debate as to whether or not this meant that Durnford inherited the order to act upon the defensive, with which Chelmsford had charged Pulleine. There can be no doubt that he did. It obviously did not occur to Lord Chelmsford that either the command of the camp, or the execution of his order to defend it, could or would be matters for debate; there was no reason why they should. Since the Zulus had last been reported as retiring, no doubt the matter seemed at the time academic. Durnford suggested that the troops should be dismissed to finish their breakfast, and he and Pulleine repaired to the latter's tent to have something to eat themselves.

They had barely finished their brief meal when a third trooper came galloping in from the vedette on the Nqutu. There were Zulus on the plateau, he said, but whether from excitement or lack of breath after his rapid descent, the man was nearly incoherent, and Pulleine sent an officer of the NNC, Lieutenant Higginson, up the escarpment to find out precisely what had been seen. At the same time, Durnford decided to send a party of his Basutos to scout the plateau thoroughly. Captain Barton, on Durnford's staff, with Lieutenant Roberts and his troop of horse were to scour the plateau to the northwest; while Captain George Shepstone was to go with Lieutenant Raw's troop to the north-east. As they made their way up on to the plateau, they passed Higginson on his way back, carrying a written message which, though addressed to Pulleine, was passed to Durnford. In it, Durnford read that the Zulus were departing along the plateau in an easterly direction – that is, towards Chelmsford and his force.

An unpleasant thought entered Durnford's mind. Chelmsford, he believed, as did everyone else in the camp, had gone off to relieve Dartnell and, in so doing, to confront the main *impi* at the far end of the plain, beyond Itelezi. That being the case, the general could well do without a fresh force of Zulus arriving to reinforce the enemy or, even worse, threatening his rear and getting astride his line of communication with Isandhlwana.

Durnford decided that there was only one course of action open to him; while Raw and Roberts drove the Zulus along the edge of the plateau, he would sally out across the plain with the rest of the troops he had brought with him from Rorke's Drift. In this way, he hoped, the Zulus would be caught between the two forces, or at least be prevented from effecting a union with the main *impi*. In this scheme there was one serious flaw: Durnford had no idea of the strength of the Zulus on the plateau.

The troops under Durnford's personal command were all

natives; it would, he considered, be preferable to stiffen them with some of the British infantry. He accordingly asked Pulleine to spare him two companies of the 24th. Pulleine demurred. The orders given by the general were to stay in the camp and defend it, not to go out chasing stray parties of Zulus. But he was in a difficult position. Durnford was his senior and Pulleine could not compel him to obey orders he felt to be binding upon himself. Durnford pointed out that the Zulus were retreating, and Pulleine agreed to give him two companies of the 24th, if he ordered it. Durnford, however, having no wish to cause any bad feeling, said that he would go with his Kaffirs only, but asked Pulleine to send out the British infantry if he found himself in difficulties; this Pulleine agreed to do.

Durnford sent Higginson galloping back to the Nqutu escarpment to find Shepstone and tell him to co-operate with the force to be moved out across the plain, and drive the Zulus along the plateau. He then suggested as a precautionary measure, in case the Zulus should elude Raw and Roberts, and slip back towards Isandhlwana, that a reinforcement should be sent to support the NNC company on the spur. Pulleine accordingly despatched Captain C. W. Cavaye with 'A' Company, 1st/24th, up to the spur to a position about 1,000 yards from the camp. Here Cavaye spread his men out to the left of the NNC position, and sent Lieutenant E. Dyson with a platoon another 500 yards to the left. Having made these arrangements, Durnford led his men out of the camp at about 11am, to carry out his plan.

To begin with, Durnford kept to the track by which Lord Chelmsford had marched out to the relief of Dartnell earlier that morning, but after passing the conical kopje he veered away to the left, that is, towards the Nqutu escarpment. Russell's rocket battery, with Captain Nourse's 'D' Company of the 1st/3rd NNC, soon began to fall behind the mounted men, and their line of march took them farther still to the north, and nearer the hills. The landscape was empty: there was no movement that Durnford could see, either upon the plain or on the rim of the plateau.

Up on the plateau, Durnford's four officers and their mounted Basutos had lost touch with the Zulus, whose presence had been the cause of the reconnaissance, so while Barton and Roberts pushed along the edge of the escarpment, keeping pace with Durnford out on the plain, Shepstone and Raw ordered their troopers to fan out and scour the ground to the north-east. Soon, a small party of Zulus was seen, driving some livestock along, and Raw's Basutos gave chase. One of them, outstripping his comrades, galloped up a rise and reined in suddenly at the edge of a ravine which had been hidden from view.

Below him, crouching in silence on the floor of the rocky valley and stretching as far as he could see, were more than 20,000 Zulu warriors. He had found the *impi*.

The solitary Basuto and the Zulu host stared at each other for a moment in mutual astonishment. Then the horseman turned and fled, and the Zulus leaped to their feet. Every one of them must have realised that there was no question of waiting for the 23rd, now that their whereabouts had been discovered. Without pausing for orders, the *impi* surged out of the ravine, spread out, and started for the lip of the plateau at a trot.

The battle of Isandhlwana had begun.

Shepstone saw the Zulus coming, spread out on a front almost a mile across. There could be no question of driving *them* along the plateau to the east. Sending Trooper Whitelaw, of the Natal Carbineers, from the vedette down the escarpment to warn Durnford of the danger, he ordered Raw and Roberts to fall back upon the spur as slowly as possible, keeping up as heavy a fire as their natives could manage in order to gain as much time as possible. He then galloped back to warn Pulleine at the camp, pausing to inform Cavaye and Dyson on the spur as he passed.

Shepstone, like the messenger who arrived when the first alarm had sounded at breakfast time, was practically incoherent by the time he reached Pulleine's tent. As he did so, the men under Dyson and Cavaye opened fire on the *impi*. While he was collecting himself, Captain Gardiner and Major Smith rode in with Chelmsford's order to Pulleine to strike camp and move to join him. It was an inopportune moment; Pulleine was perplexed as to what he should do. Here was Shepstone babbling about an enormous force of Zulus on the plateau, and there was certainly heavy firing from the spur, despite the fact that the main *impi* was supposed to be miles away to the east. So Pulleine sent his second note to Chelmsford, stating that he could not move for the present. The horseman sent to deliver this message did not know how fortunate he was, as he rode out of the camp.

It was now about noon. The bugles again rang out the alarm and the troops once more assembled in front of the tents. The reports received from the outposts on the plateau earlier in the morning had given the impression that the Zulus there numbered a few hundred, perhaps, but no more. It is clear that Shepstone, despite his excitement or perhaps because of it, failed to convey to Pulleine the urgency of the situation and that the force now bearing rapidly down on the camp was the main *impi*. Nothing but Pulleine's failure to realise this could account for what he now did.

Had he, in the brief breathing space left to him, withdrawn 'A' Company from the spur and formed the British infantry into a square beneath the hill, with the NNC and the mounted irregulars in the centre, he would in all probability have beaten off the attack and his men would have lived to fight another day. But, not thinking the Zulus to be in any real strength, Pulleine decided instead to reinforce 'A' Company with 'F' Company, 1st/24th, under Captain W. E. Mostyn.

In the camp there was still no sense of alarm. The enemy being fired at from the spur were still invisible from the tent area below. Captain Essex, one of the five officers to survive the fast approaching disaster, was in his tent writing letters when his sergeant came to report that the company on the spur was engaged. Essex, with his field-glasses, went outside to look, and took his revolver with him, 'but did not trouble to put on my sword, as I thought nothing of the matter and expected to be back in half an hour to complete my letters'.*

By the time Mostyn got his men into position between Cavaye and Dyson, the Natal Native Contingent to their right had already seen enough of their dreaded foe and had taken it upon themselves to retire to the camp. Although the mounted Basutos had now fallen back on the infantry position and were adding their fire to that of 'A' and 'F' Companies, it was clear that the men on the spur would be unable to do more than

* Essex later gave evidence before the court of inquiry.

hinder the advance of the huge *impi*; stopping it was out of the question. So, maintaining a heavy fire, Mostyn and Cavaye began to withdraw in good order, Roberts and Raw following. Pulleine now took Captain R. Younghusband's 'C' Company out of the line in front of the tents and sent him to reinforce Mostyn and Cavaye, thus compounding the error of sending them out in the first place. 'C' Company took up a position to the left of Cavaye. Between them the three companies now occupied a 600-yard front facing the spur, and about 200 yards to the north of the camp.

At about this time, the third messenger (sent by Gardiner, not Pulleine) left the camp to find Lord Chelmsford, bearing the note which reached Clery, containing the words '... Shepstone has come in for reinforcements and reports that the Zulus are falling back'. It was a curious note to send at that particular moment. Like the two preceding messages, it failed to convey any sense of urgency or any suggestion that the approaching Zulu force was the main *impi*. It is difficult to guess where Gardiner got the idea that the Zulus were retreating, since they were still not visible from the camp, and the infantry on the spur were withdrawing, hotly engaged. Again, one is left to assume either that Shepstone had not conveyed the idea that the Zulus he had seen formed part of the *impi*, or that he was simply not believed. Also, the message implies that the action had become general, whereas only three infantry companies and the mounted natives had so far fired a shot.

With the three infantry companies posted to the north of the camp, facing the spur down which they had retreated, the defences of the rest of the camp were stretched perilously thin, for Pulleine, in his ignorance of the true situation, had still not drawn in his line to form a compact defensive position. The three remaining British companies were spread out on a frontage of more than half a mile, facing the plain. On the right, with his right resting on the track, was Lieutenant C. D. Pope with 'G' Company, 2nd/24th. To his left was Captain Wardell's 'H' Company, and next to them, 'E' Company under Lieutenant F. P. Porteous. Between the three companies were gaps of 200 yards, and between Porteous and Cavaye, facing to the north of the camp, yawned a gap 300 yards wide.

In this latter gap the ground rose slightly, and here Stuart Smith and Curling set up their two guns, covering the Nqutu escarpment.

The mounted irregulars, whose principal functions were to scout or to pursue a beaten enemy, and who were not expected to stand and fight in a defensive battle, had taken up a position five or six hundred yards behind Pope's company by the wagon park. The Natal Kaffirs, of doubtful utility in an emergency, were not expected to fight defensively either, and four of Lonsdale's companies, and two of Durnford's, which had been left in the camp, had settled down uneasily right in the middle of it, behind Wardell's men. For some unknown reason, two NNC companies, one of which had been on out-post duty and the other of which had fallen back from the spur, now found themselves in a position 200 yards in advance of the gap between Porteous and Cavaye, and in front of the guns. It was not only a hazardous situation: it was also a position of critical importance in the British line of defence, since it formed the angle between the three infantry companies facing east across the plain, and those defending the northern sector of the camp. Either by an oversight, or by design, the two native companies were left where they were. So stood Pulleine's force, awaiting they knew not what. It was a dangerously weak disposition.

Durnford, meanwhile unaware of these developments, was far out on the empty plain, beyond the conical kopje, with Russell's rocket battery and its escort to his left. Suddenly he heard a shout, and saw Whitelaw, whom Shepstone had sent to alert him, pounding across the plain. But the message was hardly necessary, for there on the rim of the plateau, and already spilling down the escarpment and spreading over the plain, was the *impi*, the deadly horns extending as it came.

Nobody who survived the day can have forgotten the sight the *impi* now presented. Something between 20,000 and 25,000 warriors were extended at regular intervals, hundreds of yards deep, across a front of almost two miles, stretching from the spur above the camp to far beyond the kopje on the plain. The hills and plain were literally black with Zulus, rolling forward with all the relentless power of the incoming tide and with fearful swiftness in a vast crescent formation.

Durnford, appreciating the danger of being encircled and cut off from the camp, began to retire his mounted men at once. Nearer the plateau, Russell too had seen the oncoming host, and his nine men quickly set up one of the troughs from which the rockets – which were hand-lit – were fired. At the best of times these rockets were inaccurate and inefficient, their chief value when used against savages lying in the noise, smoke and sparks they emitted. Russell had time to fire only one before the *impi* was upon him. He and six of his men died on the spot. Three others, wounded, lay still whilst the Zulu tide swept past, and then miraculously managed to crawl away unseen. The NNC company under Captain Nourse, which was supposed to be acting as the rocket battery's escort, had fallen way behind, and Nourse succeeded in bringing his men back to the camp where he joined the two NNC companies at the angle between Porteous and Cavaye.

There was nothing Durnford could do to help Russell. Indeed, Russell's destruction imperilled his own position still further, for the Zulus were now swiftly moving around his left flank, while to his right, masses of warriors were spread out across the track. Keeping up a heavy fire, Durnford's Basutos retired in good order until they reached the big donga which ran across the plain parallel to the front of the camp. Here Durnford decided to make a stand.

The donga, some twenty yards wide at this point, was sufficiently deep to shelter a crouching man. Lining the eastern lip, Durnford's men, now joined by some of the Colonial Horse from the camp, maintained a withering fire. Durnford strode up and down the donga crying, 'Fire, my boys! Well done, my boys!' exposing himself carelessly, and laughing and talking continuously to encourage his men. The Basutos sometimes had difficulties in extracting the spent cases from their carbines, and went to Durnford and the other Europeans for help, but gradually their fire became so telling that the Zulu rush slackened and then ceased for a time, the warriors in front of the donga waiting for the left horn to continue its encircling movement. Before the donga the Zulu dead already lay thick on the ground, and the bodies put Brickhill, Pulleine's interpreter, in mind of masses of peppercorns.

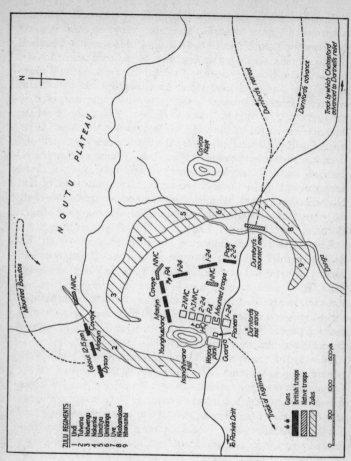

ZULU REGIMENTS
1 Undi
2 Tulwana
3 Nodwengu
4 Nokenke
5 Umcityu
6 Umbonga
7 Uve
8 Nkobamkosi
9 Nbonumbi

Guns
British troops
Native troops
Zulus

3 The battle of Isandhlwana

Back in the camp, Pulleine was no longer in doubt as to the nature of the force attacking him, and firing was now general all along the British perimeter. All the Zulus were by this time off the plateau, and were arrayed in a continuous line from the spur to a position overlapping Durnford's right. As they came steadily on, the Zulu horde gave vent not to loud cheering or war-cries, but, more sinister, a low murmuring reminiscent of the humming of a gigantic swarm of bees. Then, slowly, their advance was halted by the weight of fire poured into them from the defensive line, and for a space the battle was static.

On the northern sector of the perimeter, the three companies under Mostyn, Cavaye and Younghusband were directing their fire against the warriors of the right horn, composed of the Nodwengu regiment, identified by their white shields marked with large black spots, and the iSangqu, 'The White Tails'. Here, where the warriors had come down from the spur, they had succeeded in approaching to within 300 yards of the British infantry. At that distance the fire was so intense that dozens of warriors fell with every volley; so they had lain down and were crawling slowly closer between the volleys.

At the angle defended by the two exposed NNC companies, the situation was already ugly. The Kaffirs, poor shots at the best of times, had few rifles and little ammunition between them. Their European officers and NCOs were firing away, manfully with their carbines and revolvers, but against such overwhelming numbers they could make little impression.

Now that the range had shortened, the two guns were firing case (a type of shrapnel), but were doing very little execution. The Zulus had noticed that, the second before the guns fired, the gunners stood clear of their pieces. When they saw this happen the warriors threw themselves to the ground with cries of *'uMoya*!' – 'Air!' and the shot tore harmlessly over their heads. Here, in the right centre of the *impi*, the Nokenke, 'The Long Horns', with their black shields, and the Ukhandempemvu, 'The Sharp Red Stake' (i.e. a thing pointed at both ends), and part of the umCityu, were slowly gaining ground. If the Kaffirs, by now badly frightened, broke, a fatal gap would be created between the two groups of British infantry, through which the Zulus would surge unimpeded.

Pope, Porteous and Wardell were firing away at large masses of the umCityu and umHlanga, but their three companies were stretched out on a front twice as long as that defended by the three companies on the north of the perimeter, and here the Zulus managed to get closer before being halted.

To the right, out in front of Pope's company, Durnford and his mounted men were still holding the bulk of the left horn in front of the donga. Here, the warriors of the Ngobamakosi, 'The Humblers of Kings', with their red and black spotted shields, and the uVe, 'The Birds that settled on the Royal Lion', could make no progress. To the extreme left of the *impi*, the Mbonambi, 'The Beholders of Sorrow', the only Zulu regiment permitted to wear the plumes of the royal lauri bird, were slowly working their way around Durnford's right.

For a time it seemed as if the battle was going well. The volume of fire, at close range, from the British line was intense, and the ground beyond the perimeter was littered with hundreds of dead or mortally wounded warriors. The Zulus had few firearms, and were inexpert in the use of those they had, and they could not as yet close to assegai range. The volley firing was a fearful experience, which many remembered years after the war. The front ranks of the *impi* began to waver, but at the critical moment a great voice from the ranks cried, 'Cetewayo did not tell us to run away,' and the mass of warriors steadied.

The only place where the Zulus were still making rapid progress was far to the right of where the Nodwengu and iSangqu had come down the spur. The Undi corps and the uThulwana had come down from the plateau at its far western end, and then, turning south, had moved behind Isandhlwana hill towards the track. Here they were in a position to cut off the British line of retreat and, in conjunction with the Mbonambi in the left horn, to complete the encirclement of the camp.

For perhaps a quarter of an hour the vast *impi* was held at bay by the terrible volley firing of the British regulars, and by Durnford's gallant Basuto and colonial horsemen. But then, little by little, the shooting began to slacken and falter: ammunition in the firing-line was running low.

Cavaye's company, the first to be engaged, had marched up

the spur with seventy rounds of Martini-Henry* ammunition each; but they had now been firing for almost an hour. Mostyn's and Younghusband's troops had only been shooting for half that time, as had the three companies facing the plain, but they had started out with fewer rounds per man. The situation hardly constituted an emergency, however, for besides the regimental reserves there were nearly half a million rounds of ammunition in the wagon park. As supplies began to dwindle, the company commanders had sent back for more.

The first and second battalions of the 24th Regiment had separate reserves, packed in separate wagons. The reserve for the 2nd/24th, of which only Pope's 'G' Company was present, was under the supervision of Quartermaster Bloomfield, and was situated behind the 2nd/24th tent area, in the centre of the camp, more than 1,000 yards from Pope's position. The reserve of the 1st/24th, under Quartermaster Pullen, was even farther away from the troops it was to serve, at the southern end of the tent line.

But it was not only the distance of the reserve ammunition from the firing line which was causing difficulty. When the runners from the three 1st/24th companies on the north side of the camp began to come in for fresh supplies, Bloomfield, who was nearest, refused them, sending them another 500 yards to the south, to their own quartermaster, Pullen. Bloomfield undoubtedly felt that it would have been an infringement of the regulations by which his life was governed to issue ammunition to a unit other than his own.

Durnford, too, had sent several natives back to the camp to

* The Martini-Henry rifle was introduced into the British Army in 1871. The action was invented by an American, but improved by an Austrian, von Martini, and was coupled to a seven-grooved barrel designed by an Edinburgh gunsmith, Alexander Henry. It was a single-shot weapon operated by a lever situated behind the trigger guard which opened the breech, cocked the firing-pin and extracted the empty case. The cartridge it fired was invented by Col Boxer, whose name it bore, in 1867. It was of ·450 calibre and fired a 480-grain bullet propelled by 83 grains of powder. The case was made of thin coiled brass. It was a fine combination of rifle and cartridge, but suffered from two faults: the thin brass cases sometimes caused jamming when the rifle was hot; and the deep lands of the rifling quickly fouled with the lead bullets, causing the weapon to kick viciously.

replenish his supplies, but neither Pullen nor Bloomfield would part with any of their precious reserves, every box of which was accountable, to any Kaffirs, who returned to Durnford empty handed. He then sent Lieutenant Henderson back; but he too was refused by the quartermasters, and was unable to locate the proper reserve for the Basutos in the dozens of wagons in the park.

There was another difficulty: the lids of the ammunition boxes were held in place by six screws and, by some oversight, there was a dearth of screwdrivers. More precious moments were wasted while men prised the lids off with bayonets and knives.

Lieutenant Smith-Dorrien, who after delivering the order to Durnford had breakfasted with the officers at Rorke's Drift and then made his way back to the camp, was all too well aware of the grave situation rapidly developing. Having no specific duties of his own, he organised some of the camp-followers to rip open some of the 2nd Battalion's ammunition boxes and distribute their precious contents to the runners from the firing-line. Bloomfield was horrified.

'For heaven's sake don't take that, man, for it belongs to our battalion!' he said.

Smith-Dorrien, quite out of patience, snapped back: 'Hang it all, you don't want a requisition now, do you?' and went on with the work.*

Smith-Dorrien was not the only worried man by this time. A colonial wagon conductor remarked to him: 'The game is up. If I had a good horse, I would ride straight for Maritzburg.'

At last, the inevitable happened: Durnford's men ran out of ammunition and could prolong their resistance no longer. Seizing their horses, they hurriedly left the shelter of the donga and rode back past the right flank of Pope's company, to join the other mounted men assembled on the nek. The Ngoba-makosi and the Mbonambi, now freed from the deadly fire which had pinned them down, leaped to their feet and bounded forward across the donga.

'G' Company was outflanked by this advance and wheeled to meet the threat, thereby taking the pressure off the Zulus to

* Smith-Dorrien, Gen Sir H. *Memories of Forty-Eight Years' Service.*

their front. As the left horn of the *impi* surged forward, the great host of warriors, till now silent save for the low murmuring, began to stamp on the ground and beat upon their shields with their assegais, and then the dreaded war-cry *uSuthu!** broke out and was taken up all along the line by more than 20,000 voices.

Encouraged by the movement of the left horn, the warriors of the chest and right horn swept forward. It was too much for the two NNC companies at the angle: they turned and fled headlong towards the camp and the nek, across which they imagined lay salvation. Their white officers and NCOs were powerless to stop them. Smith and Curling hastily limbered up the guns and fell back into the camp also. It was at about this time that Lord Chelmsford, ten miles away, was looking at the camp through his field glasses, and seeing the tents still standing was assured everything was all right.

The movement was disastrous. The departure of the NNC left a gap 300 yards wide between Cavaye's 'A' Company and Mostyn's 'F' Company, fighting on the northern side of the perimeter, and Porteous, with 'E' Company, and Wardell's 'H' Company, facing the plain. The Zulus were quick to exploit their opportunity. Hundreds of warriors of the umCityu, Nokenke and Ukhandempemvu regiments came pouring through the gap, outflanking the infantry on either side.

From this point onwards all order and cohesion in the defence of the camp were lost, and the battle dissolved into a series of bitter and isolated struggles, some conducted by companies and platoons, some by smaller groups of men, some by individuals, each red-coat or group of red-coats the centre of a black storm of yelling, stabbing Zulus.

'A' and 'F' Companies, busy firing at the warriors to their front, were fallen upon from behind by the Zulus who had burst through the gap left by the Kaffirs. Taken by surprise, with Zulus before and behind them and without even time to fix bayonets, they died where they stood, hacked to pieces in a few moments. There were no survivors; Cavaye and Mostyn fell with their men.

* The title of the faction of which Cetewayo had been leader before becoming king.

With 'E' and 'H' Companies it was nearly as bad. Wardell's men had been stretched to cover the gap between their position and Pope's. There were great spaces between individual soldiers, and they, like everyone else, were short of ammunition. A great wave of the umHlanga and umCityu crashed forward and enveloped 'H' Company, assegaiing the British infantry piecemeal and, hardly pausing, swept on towards the tents, leaving a line of red-clad bodies strewn behind them.

Porteous was caught like Cavaye and Mostyn, from two sides, and 'E' Company was wiped out of existence with the same fearful thoroughness. Some of Pope's men, now isolated, lasted a little longer. They had already wheeled to deal with the rush of Ngobamakosi and Mbonambi, occasioned by the withdrawal of Durnford's force. Now the warriors who had wiped out the two companies under Wardell and Porteous turned and fell on Pope's rear. 'G' Company retreated slowly up the track, maintaining such resistance as was possible. Most of them fell in small groups, but a few, led by Pope, managed to reach the nek.

At the northernmost end of the British perimeter, Younghusband's 'C' Company was putting up a longer and better organised resistance than was taking place elsewhere, for he had had a few moments' grace. His men had time to fix their bayonets, and Younghusband withdrew them slowly between the tents and the foot of Isandhlwana, then up the side of the hill itself. Here, when all their ammunition was fired, 'C' Company held out to the last, fighting with bayonets and using their rifles as clubs. After the battle, a warrior of the Nokenke regiment stated that the last of these men in sheer desperation charged down into the press of their adversaries, who surrounded and speared them all to death.

On the nek, the last organised resistance was being slowly overcome. Here, Colonel Durnford, with fourteen Carbineers and a score of Natal Mounted Policemen – all of whom could have got away on horseback, but who chose to dismount and fight it out – died with the remains of Pope's company near by. There was, even at this stage, no *sauve qui peut* amongst the Europeans, who filled many of the Zulus with a lasting admiration. 'Ah, those red soldiers at Isandhlwana', one of them told

Captain Hallam-Parr after the war, 'how few they were, and how they fought! They fell like stones – each man in his place.'*
Another Zulu eyewitness account, given to Norris-Newman, described graphically how the colonials around Durnford died:

They threw down their guns, when their ammunition was done, and then commenced with their pistols, which they fired as long as their ammunition lasted; and then they formed a line, shoulder to shoulder, and back to back, and fought with their knives.

The *Official Narrative* records another Zulu account of Durnford's last stand:

When we closed in, we came to a mixed party of mounted and infantry men who had evidently been stopped by the end of our Horn. They numbered about a hundred. They made a desperate resistance, some firing with pistols and others using swords. I repeatedly heard the word 'fire' given by someone. But we proved too many for them, and killed them all where they stood. When all was over I had a look at these men, and I saw an officer with his arm in a sling and with a big moustache, [this was probably Durnford], surrounded by carabineers, soldiers and other men I didn't know.

At one o'clock, by some sinister coincidence, as if to augur the destruction of the British, there was a partial eclipse of the sun. 'The tumult and the firing was wonderful,' remembered one warrior; 'every warrior shouted "Usutu!" as he killed anyone,' and then, 'the sun got very dark, like night.'

Within the camp itself, amongst the tents and wagons, the scene was now one of utter chaos, as the Zulus mopped up the last pockets of resistance and started looting.

Pullen, the quartermaster of the 1st/24th, tried to rally a small group of stray soldiers and was later found with their bodies around him. Bloomfield, who had been so reluctant to issue ammunition at the moment of need, died with some others while trying to untie some boxes of the precious ammunition from the backs of mules.

Behind the officers' tents a determined stand was made by seventy or so men who fell where they stood under the rain of assegais. A little way off, Colour Sergeant Wolf gathered twenty

* Hallam-Parr, Capt H. *A Sketch of the Kaffir and Zulu Wars.*

men about him; his body, surrounded by theirs, was found with a litter of dead Zulus round them. The hands of mauy of these men were found to have burns across the palms, caused by their rifle barrels overheating from the prolonged firing, before the ammunition gave out. Near Wolf's group, Captain Wardell and Lieutenant Dyer of 'H' Company, who had fought their way back to the tent area, fell.

The only bluejacket in the camp, a man from HMS *Active*, acting as Lieutenant Milne's servant, was seen with his back against a wagon wheel, furiously defending himself with his cutlass, and keeping a crowd of Zulus at bay. Then one of them crawled under the wagon from behind and plunged a spear into his back.

One of the colonial horsemen put his back against a boulder near the hospital tents and, well supplied with cartridges, shot any warrior who approached. His body was found later with about a hundred spent cases lying about him, his revolver empty, and his bloody hunting-knife still clenched in his hand.

Another man – possibly Captain Younghusband – kept up a prolonged resistance from a wagon, firing away until his ammunition was exhausted. Then he fought on with his bayonet, transfixing any Zulu who came too near. Finally, somebody with a gun shot him.

Some time after the Zulus had burst through the defensive line and the slaughter amongst the tents had started, Pulleine had taken the Queen's Colour of the 1st/24th (the regimental colour was back at Helpmakaar), and given it to Lieutenant Teignmouth Melvill, adjutant of the 1st Battalion, ordering him to take it to a place of safety. Pulleine and Melvill then shook hands, and Melvill rode off across the nek, over which a stream of fugitives was already fleeing. Pulleine must have been killed shortly afterwards.

It was by now about 1.30, barely an hour and a half since the *impi* had come into view, and there was only one man left alive in the camp. This soldier, whose name and regiment are unknown, retreated alone up the side of Isandhlwana, taking with him a good supply of ammunition, and established himself in a recess in the rocks. He was very cool, and husbanded his cartridges, taking deliberate aim and killing every warrior who came near. This went on until late in the afternoon, when a number of Zulus fired simultaneously into the recess, killing the last British soldier to die at Isandhlwana.

Everyone still alive, black and white alike, was by now in full flight across the nek, in the direction of Rorke's Drift and, as they thought, safety. But it was not to be, for the Undi and uThulwana regiments, who had moved behind Isandhlwana at the start of the battle and taken no part in the fighting in the camp, were across the track, while the Mbonambi of the left horn had almost succeeded in effecting a junction with them in order to close the trap completely. There was still a small gap left between the two Zulu wings, to the left of the track, and through this opening went the survivors, pell-mell. It was quite literally a question of the devil take the hindmost.

The terrain between the nek and the Buffalo, three and a half miles away, was cut by gullies and strewn with rocks and boulders, and in places overgrown with patches of bush. On ground such as this, the Zulus could run as fast as the horses of those lucky enough to be mounted, and they were soon amongst the fugitives, pulling men from their saddles, stabbing and thrusting with their assegais in every direction.

When the two NNC companies at the angle had given way, Smith and Curling had limbered up the two guns and started to retire into the camp. As the withdrawal developed into a rout, the two officers and the gunners fought their way through the mass of terrified Kaffirs, who tried to cling to the guns, and over the nek. Half a mile from the nek a deep gully with precipitous sides cut across the line of retreat. Somehow or other the two guns were taken this far, but their weight rolling downhill pushed the teams over the edge of the gully, where the horses, hanging in their harness, were speared. Major Smith, by this time wounded, got as far as the river, where he was caught and killed. Lieutenant Curling was one of the few lucky ones to make good his escape and reach Helpmakaar. The Zulus towed the guns away, by hand, and dragged them right to Ulundi.

Lieutenant Melvill, with the Queen's Colour, had by this time been joined by Lieutenant Coghill, Colonel Glyn's orderly officer, and the two had reached a point between the gully and the Buffalo when Paul Brickhill, the interpreter, came pounding along. 'Mr Brickhill', asked Melvill, 'have you seen anything of my sword back there?' Brickhill said that he had not, and dashed on. He too made his escape.

Melvill and Coghill were not so fortunate. They rode as far as the river – to Fugitives' Drift as it came to be called – and plunged in. Coghill got across to the Natal bank, but Melvill, encumbered with the heavy Colour, was swept from his saddle by the force of the water. This must have been at about ten past two, for it was at that time that Melvill's watch was later found to have stopped. Some way down the stream was a rock, on to which Lieutenant Higginson of the NNC was clinging, and Melvill, still clutching grimly to the Colour, caught on to it. Then both men were washed off the rock and downstream again. The Zulus were by this time at the river in strength, spearing those on foot, intercepting the horsemen, and even dashing into the water to kill those fugitives who got thus far. Those with rifles were peppering the river and the far bank with bullets. Notwithstanding this, Coghill gallantly rode back into the Buffalo to try to rescue Melvill, but a bullet killed his horse. Melvill, who had now lost the precious Colour, Coghill and Higginson somehow reached the bank, and the latter started off to find some horses. Melvill and Coghill, nearing the end of their strength, struggled on; Coghill, with an injured knee, could not walk without assistance. Numbers of Zulus had by now crossed the river and the two officers were surrounded. Their bodies were later found with those of several dead warriors. They were buried side by side, and in 1907 were posthumously awarded the Victoria Cross. The Queen's Colour was recovered washed up on the river bank, and sent back to Helpmakaar.

Surgeon-Major Shepherd gave his life trying to save a trooper named Kelley, who had been assegaied. Shepherd was well mounted, but a Natal carbineer shouted to him to help the trooper. The surgeon dismounted to do so, and said, 'Poor fellow, too late, too late!' As Shepherd remounted, he was struck by an assegai, and fell dead. Captain George Shepstone also lost his life through a gallant disregard for danger. Having disengaged his men and brought them across the nek, he decided to go back into the camp and find Durnford. He was killed on the track on the nek.

When the two Natal Native Contingent companies at the angle bolted, two of their white officers, Lieutenants Davis and Henderson, went with them. A huge Zulu barred Davis's retreat and seized his horse's bridle. Davis lunged at the warrior with his carbine, which had a knife fixed bayonet-fashion to the barrel, but the Zulu tore it from his grasp. Davis put the spurs to his mount and galloped on. Another warrior lunged at him, but Davis pistolled the man, and the horse received the stab aimed at the rider. Davis tore on, with assegais hurtling about him, and reached the river. He rode his horse into the water and clinging to the stirrup iron was towed across to safety.

Another man who lived to tell the tale was Trooper Charles Montague Sparks of the Natal Mounted Police. At the moment the Zulus burst through the perimeter and charged towards the tents, Sparks was talking to a saddler named Pearce; they agreed that the situation looked serious; and then the black horde, yelling *Gwas Umhlongo! Gwas Inglubi!* – 'Stab the white men! Stab the pigs!' – was upon them. Pearce, however, seems to have been more frightened of his sergeant-major than of the Zulus, for when Sparks cried, 'Come back, man, let's ride off!' Pearce disappeared into his tent in order to change the bit he had for another one, saying, 'What a choking off I'll get if the SM sees me riding with a snaffle instead of the regulation bit.' Pearce failed to emerge from the tent. Sparks galloped off towards the river, which by the time he reached it was filled with the bodies of drowning, wounded and struggling men, both white and black. On the bank, amidst this scene of terror and confusion, Sparks was astounded to find another man he knew, Kincaid, sitting calmly draining the water out of his boots. Kincaid had lost his horse and so by this time had Sparks, but by a piece of miraculous good fortune they managed to catch two others, and rode to safety.*

But the most vivid of all eyewitness accounts of that nightmare flight is contained in part of a letter which Lieutenant Smith-Dorrien wrote to his father on 25 January from Rorke's Drift:

* Clements, W. H. *The Glamour and Tragedy of the Zulu War.*

At about 10.30 the Zulus were seen coming over the hills in thousands. They were in most perfect order, and seemed to be in about 20 rows of skirmishers one behind the other. They were in a semi-circle round our two flanks and in front of us and must have covered several miles of ground. Nobody knows how many there were of them, but the general idea is at least 20,000 ... Before we knew where we were they came right into the camp assegaiing everybody right and left. Everybody then who had a horse turned to fly. The enemy were going at a kind of very fast half-walk and half-run. On looking round we saw that we were completely surrounded and the road to Rorke's Drift was cut off. The place where they seemed thinnest was where we all made for. Everybody went pell-mell over ground covered with huge boulders and rocks until we got to a deep spruit or gully. How the horses got over I have no idea ... There was a poor fellow of the mounted infantry (a private) struck through the arm, who said as I passed that if I could bind up his arm and stop the bleeding he would be all right. I accordingly took out my hand-kerchief and tied up his arm. Just as I had done it, Major Smith of the Artillery came down by me wounded, saying 'For God's sake get on, man; the Zulus are on top of us.' I had done all I could for the wounded man and so turned to jump on my horse. Just as I was doing so the horse went with a bound to the bottom of the precipice, being struck with an assegai. I gave up all hope, as the Zulus were all round me, finishing off the wounded, the man I had helped and Major Smith among the number. However with the strong hope that everybody clings to that some accident would turn up, I rushed off on foot and plunged into the river, which was little better than a roaring torrent. I was being carried down stream at a tremendous pace, when a loose horse came by me and I got hold of his tail and he landed me safely on the other bank; but I was too tired to stick to him and get on his back. I got up again and rushed on and was several times knocked over by our mounted niggers, who would not get out of my way, then up a tremendous hill ... A few Zulus followed us for about three miles across the river, but they had no guns, and I had a revolver, which I kept letting them know. Also the mounted niggers stopped a little and kept firing at them. They did not come in close, and finally stopped altogether.*

Smith-Dorrien and a few others struggled into Helpmakaar, twenty miles away, at nightfall. Of the imperial officers, only

* Smith-Dorrien.

five – Smith-Dorrien, Essex, Cochrane, Curling and Gardiner – survived. They owed this to the fact that they wore their blue patrol jackets that day and not their red tunics. Before the great *impi* left Ulundi, Cetewayo had told his warriors that the soldiers they were to destroy wore red; and that the civilian element of the columns, who were of no importance, wore blue.

As the afternoon wore on, the orgy of burning, looting and mutilation of the dead at the camp-site reached a peak and slowly dwindled, as the warriors of the *impi*, bearing as much booty as they could carry, dispersed towards the hills and their own kraals. They left behind between two and three thousand of their own dead. Never before had a Zulu army sustained such casualties. 'An assegai has been thrust into the belly of the nation,' said Cetewayo when he heard the news.

As darkness fell, the only ones left alive within the camp at Isandhlwana were a few Zulus who had found enough liquor to get drunk. Scattered around the perimeter of the camp, between the tents, amongst the wagons, up on the nek and all along the fugitives' trail, lay the bodies of over 800 white soldiers and nearly 500 Natal Kaffirs. There were no wounded.

Cetewayo's warriors had at last washed their spears.

Out on the plain there was a wait while Lord Chelmsford gathered together his widely separated troops. 'While we were skirmishing in front,' the general told his exhausted men when they had assembled, 'the Zulus have taken our camp. There are 10,000 Zulus in our rear, and 20,000 in our front; we must win back to our camp tonight, and cut our way back to Rorke's Drift tomorrow.' The troops replied with a cheer, 'All right, sir; we'll do it.' It was 8pm when they reached Isandhlwana. By now darkness covered the horrors of the stricken camp: it might also, feared Chelmsford, conceal the victorious *impi*, lurking to fall upon his own force and wipe it out as well. Fires were burning on the hills around and, more ominous, the sky to the west, in the direction of Rorke's Drift, was aglow from a bigger conflagration.

Chelmsford proceeded with caution. First the four guns were unlimbered, and raked the nek with shrapnel. Then, Major Black of the 2nd/24th advanced with his three companies to take possession of the stony kopje on the south side of the track. 'No firing,' said Black, 'but only one volley, boys, and then give them the cold steel.' But the place was inhabited only by the dead; there was no opposition, and 'a ringing British cheer' announced to the general and his staff that the kopje was taken.

For a few hours, Chelmsford's demoralised troops rested on the nek, where the mutilated corpses of their late comrades lay thick in every position of death; so thick that a man could hardly lie down, or turn over without coming into contact with a body. The men were forbidden to go into the camp itself, but one or two of the officers did so.

Hamilton-Browne went to his tent, and found his servant dead, his two spare horses killed on their picket ropes and his setter bitch pinned to the ground by an assegai. Glyn, too, visited the camp, and found the bodies of Pulleine, Young-husband and Durnford, all stripped naked. The dead lay everywhere, in windrows. Every body was mutilated, with the stomach slashed open, in order, the Zulus believed, to release the spirit of the dead. Here, a ghastly circle of soldiers' heads was laid out; there, a drummer-boy hanging from a wagon by his feet, with his throat cut. A Natal mounted policeman and a Zulu lay dead, locked together as they had fallen, the policeman uppermost. Two other combatants lay close together, the Zulu with a bayonet thrust through his skull and the white man with an assegai plunged into his chest. A soldier of the 24th lay speared through the back, with two other assegais by him, the blades bent double. It was the same all over the field. Norris-Newman, the newspaper correspondent, also inspected the camp:

The corpses of our poor soldiers, whites and natives, lay thick upon the ground in clusters, together with the dead and muti-lated horses, oxen and mules, shot and stabbed in every position and manner; and the whole intermingled with the fragments of our Commissariat wagons, broken and wrecked, and rifled of their contents, such as flour, sugar, tea, biscuits, mealies, oats etc., the debris being scattered about and wasted as in pure wantonness on the ground.*

* Norris-Newman, C. L. *In Zululand with the British.*

Before first light on the morning of the 23rd, Lord Chelmsford marched the survivors of the Central Column off the nek, away from Isandhlwana and in the direction of Rorke's Drift and Natal.

Chapter four
The Defence of
Rorke's Drift

January 22 had begun quietly at Rorke's Drift. Just before dawn, Lieutenant Horace Smith-Dorrien splashed across the ford and rode into the post: he had been in the saddle since shortly after midnight with Crealock's order to hurry Durnford's troops up to Isandhlwana. Durnford's camp was on the Zulu side of the Buffalo; the colonel had just ridden off to Helpmakaar with forty men of the Edendale contingent to find additional transport. A messenger was sent galloping after him. On his return, Durnford led his force of 250 troopers of the Natal Native Horse, a rocket battery and three companies of the 1st/3rd NNC towards the main camp at Isandhlwana.

As he ate breakfast with the officers at the Drift, Smith-Dorrien, who was in charge of the wagons with No 3 Column, said that a big fight was expected. After breakfast, Lieutenant Chard, one of the officers at the post, sought permission of Major Spalding, the Deputy Assistant Quartermaster General, commanding Rorke's Drift and the section of the frontier adjacent to it, to ride up to Isandhlwana to visit another officer, and departed at once. Smith-Dorrien, after borrowing eleven rounds of revolver ammunition from Lieutenant Gonville Bromhead, in command of 'B' Company, the 2nd/24th, rode off after Chard to collect fifty or so wagons due to return to Rorke's Drift.

The busiest men that morning were Surgeon-Major James Henry Reynolds and three members of the Army Medical Department, tending thirty-five sick men and a wounded Zulu. Rorke's Drift had been run as a mission station by a Swede, Otto Witt. Its buildings consisted of a mud-brick, thatched, house, which now served as a makeshift field hospital, and a stone barn, in use as a commissariat store. The curious construction of the hospital building made Reynolds' task no easier: five of the eleven rooms had no connecting doors and opened only on to the outside; five also had no windows. The sick men were in five small rooms grouped around the veranda, only one of which communicated directly with the front of the house; the other four had doors giving on to the back. Reynolds had set up his dispensary just off the veranda, and was keeping the two front rooms as dressing stations.

Reynolds' patients, who represented most units of the Central Column, were either sick or had been injured in accidents. Only three – Corporal Friederich Schiess, a Swiss, and Corporal Mayer, both of the NNC, and the Zulu – were wounded. They had all received leg wounds at the storming of Sirayo's kraal. The Zulu, one of Sirayo's warriors, was in a room by himself. All the sick men lay on straw palliasses, with the exception of Sergeant Maxfield who, delirious with fever, tossed about on Witt's bed.

Lieutenant Chard returned to Rorke's Drift at about midday, having passed Durnford's force and then Smith-Dorrien on their way up to the camp. He had reached Isandhlwana when the men were under arms after the first alarm, and left the camp when the second messenger from the Nqutu escarpment had ridden in to say that a body of Zulus was moving north-west. It was possible, Chard thought, that they might make for Rorke's Drift.

After lunch, Witt, the missionary, George Smith, the chaplain, and Reynolds, accompanied by a private named Wall, set out to climb the Oscarberg hill behind the post, armed with a telescope to see if they could discover the source of distant gunfire that could now be heard.

At about 2pm Major Spalding decided to ride into Helpmakaar: the Drift's garrison was to be augmented by a company of the 1st/24th, which was two days overdue, and he was anxious to find out the reason for the delay. Spalding was expected back by nightfall; meanwhile command of the little mission devolved upon Lieutenant Chard, who was three years senior to Lieutenant Bromhead. Reynolds as a surgeon was not eligible for a fighting command. After Spalding rode off, Chard made his way down to the drift to see how the work on the approaches to the ferry was progressing. Sergeant Milne, of the 2nd/3rd Buffs, was there, supervising half-a-dozen Kaffirs, and so was the ferry-man, a civilian named Daniels, in case the two punts and the ox teams were required.

Then, at about 3.15, two horsemen, shouting as they came, galloped into view on the Zulu bank and splashed into the drift. They were Lieutenant James Adendorff, of Lonsdale's regiment, NNC, and a carbineer. They bore appalling news. A huge Zulu *impi* had fallen on the camp at Isandhlwana and butchered the troops there almost to a man. One horn of the *impi* was advancing swiftly on Rorke's Drift. Adendorff said he would stay to assist in the defence of the mission, while the carbineer, who not surprisingly 'was in his shirt-sleeves', galloped on to warn the inhabitants and garrison of Helpmakaar.

Unknown to Chard, Bromhead almost simultaneously received the same terrible information in a message brought by one of the Edendale men from Captain Gardiner, of the 14th Hussars. Gardiner had escaped across Fugitives' Drift and was making his way to Helpmakaar with Captain Essex and Lieutenant Cochrane. Bromhead ordered the tents to be struck and the sick to be loaded into the wagons, in case a retreat should be necessary, and sent a message down to Chard, asking him to return at once to the camp.

When Chard arrived a few moments later, he and Bromhead held a brief consultation. Should they try to hold the ill-prepared buildings, or retreat immediately and attempt to reach Helpmakaar? In reality, there was only one course of action open to the two young officers, as Dalton, the Commissariat Department officer and a former sergeant-major in an infantry regiment, pointed out. They had to stand and fight. Even if the sick were got across the river in the wagons before the *impi* arrived, the Zulus would rapidly overtake them on the road, and in the open they would stand even less chance than they now had. Besides, if the Drift were abandoned, a large quantity of stores would certainly fall to the enemy. Chard, therefore, gave orders for the immediate fortification of the post and, in Private Henry Hook's words, 'that we were never to say "die" or "surrender"!'*

* Hook, H. 'How They Held Rorke's Drift.' *The Royal Magazine* (February 1905).

The mission station was ill suited to a defensive role, especially at short notice and with the number of men at Chard's disposal. There were ninety-eight NCOs and men of Bromhead's 'B' Company, a few men of the 1st/24th and some from other units of the Central Column. There was also an unattached company of the Natal Native Contingent, about 300 strong, under Captain George Stephenson. In all, the force numbered only about 400 men, excluding the sick.

It was clearly necessary to try to defend the house and the barn, but as these were nearly thirty yards apart this would make for a very thinly defended perimeter.

Between the house and an orchard some thirty yards in front of it ran a ledge of rock, which meant that the buildings were three or four feet above the level of the orchard. Below the ledge a patch of bush had been left uncleared. Both the orchard and the bush would make good cover for the Zulus, but there was neither time nor labour available to clear them.

While Bromhead was supervising the loopholing and barricading of the buildings, Dalton was busy emptying the store of bags of mealies and boxes of biscuits and tinned meat. With the mealie bags, weighing about 200lb apiece, and some of the biscuit boxes, which weighed a hundredweight, Chard started the men building a wall across the north side of the mission. From the north-west corner of the hospital, the wall reached out to the rock ledge, which here gave it valuable extra height. Then it ran across the front of the hospital and the space between the two buildings, till it joined the corner of the well-built cattle kraal which in turn abutted on to the north-east corner of the storehouse. This section of the defences, about chest high, faced the orchard and the patch of uncut bush, as well as a wall which Witt had begun to build but which there was no time to demolish. The mealie-bag wall on the south side was shorter, running only from the north-west corner of the store to the nearest, that is the south-east, corner of the hospital. The rooms on the south side of the hospital were thus open to direct attack, and were defensible only from within. Two wagons standing between the buildings were incorporated into the south wall, with biscuit boxes placed between the wheels.

While this work was in progress, Chard rode down to the

river to see that the punts were correctly tied up in mid-stream, and to hurry the men back to the post. Sergeant Milne and Daniels, the civilian punt-man, bravely volunteered to try to hold the drift with a few men on the punts, but the craft afforded no cover from rifle fire or assegais and Chard refused the offer, for the attempt would have been suicidal.

By the time Chard had galloped back to the post, it was about 3.30pm. Work on the barricades was in feverish progress. A few moments later, an officer of Durnford's mounted Kaffirs arrived, with a troop of his men, and asked for orders. Chard, greatly encouraged by this timely reinforcement, requested the officer to send a detachment to cover the punts, and to throw out patrols in the direction from which the Zulus were expected. They were then to fall back as the *impi* came on, and assist in the defence of the mission buildings. Two troopers of the Natal Mounted Police and a Natal carbineer, exhausted and minus most of their equipment, rode by without stopping, and disappeared in the direction of Helpmakaar. They had seen what the Zulu hordes had done at Isandhlwana, and did not give much for the chances of the defenders of Rorke's Drift.

Events now began to happen quickly. Surgeon-Major Reynolds, seeing horsemen approaching the drift and thinking they might require medical treatment, had descended the Oscarberg, but the chaplain, the missionary Witt and Private Wall remained at the summit. From there they could observe several miles of the Buffalo, down to a bend which hid Fugitives' Drift. Suddenly, as they watched, the *impi* came into sight on the Zulu bank of the river. The warriors, linked arm in arm to resist the swift current, surged across in a human chain on to the Natal side. Here they rested and indulged in their favourite pastime of taking snuff. Then they began slowly moving towards the mission station. A scouting party broke away, but the main body – some 4,500 strong – suddenly started into a trot. Smith, Witt and Wall fled down the hillside, the latter yelling, 'Here they come, black as hell and thick as grass!'

Witt, the missionary, horrified at the destruction of his property, and hearing of the disaster that had befallen the Central Column, decided that discretion was the better part of valour, and departed in the direction of Helpmakaar. (He was later to

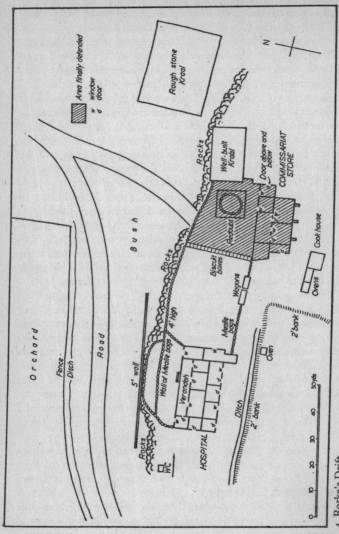

4 Rorke's Drift

set up as a lecturer in England, claiming to have been present not only at Rorke's Drift, but at Isandhlwana as well.)

Whether unnerved by Witt's hasty retreat or by the thought of the oncoming Zulus, Durnford's mounted natives, after firing off a few shots, at about 4.20pm also rode off towards Helpmakaar. Their officer, crying that he could no longer control them, followed. These desertions, which reduced the garrison's strength by about 100 men, proved altogether too much for Stephenson and his 300 Natal Kaffirs, who also bolted. Such behaviour was more than some of the British troops could stand: a volley crashed out, and Stephenson's European sergeant fell dead, shot in the back. After the battle, Chard made no mention of this shooting in his official report, and laconically stated: 'About the same time Captain Stephenson's detachment of Natal Native Contingent left us, as did that officer himself.'

Whereas before, Chard's position had been desperate, it now verged on the hopeless. Within a few moments his force had been reduced to a total of 139 of all ranks, of whom only 104 were fit for duty. Obviously the original perimeter, embracing the hospital, was now too long to defend. The sick would have to be evacuated and the defensible area of the post reduced.

There was still a heap of mealie bags and biscuit boxes lying outside the storehouse, and Chard immediately set some of the men to work in running a wall from the north-west corner of the store to the front wall along the ledge, halving the original perimeter. Even as this work was begun, the leading warriors of the *impi* came into sight round the western spur of the Oscarberg. A volley of shots rang out from the hospital loopholes and the south wall. It was just an hour and a quarter since Adendorff had brought the warning. The battle of Rorke's Drift had begun.

The *impi* that threw itself upon the little garrison was composed of three regiments. The inDlu-yengwe, something over a thousand strong, was composed of unmarried men about thirty-three years of age. The other two regiments – the uThulwana, one of the Undi corps units, and the uDloko – wore the *isiCoco* symbol of married men. The uThulwana, sometimes known as the Amasoka, whose name signified 'Those who cover looted cattle with dust', was Cetewayo's own regiment. Raised by

Mpande, its headquarters was at the royal kraal at Ulundi. The men, who bore white shields, were forty-five years old and 1,500 strong. The uDloko, whose name was derived from the plume worn in their head-dress, carried red shields spotted with white; they were slightly younger – about forty-one. With 2,000 warriors, it was the strongest of the three regiments. The *impi* was led by Dabulamanzi, Cetewayo's brother, riding a white horse. When the main Zulu force had swept down from the Nqutu plateau towards the camp at Isandhlwana, he had led the Undi and the uDloko behind Isandhlwana hill to cut off any retreat towards Rorke's Drift along the track over the nek.

Since Cetewayo was said to have forbidden any advance over the border into Natal, it may be that the attack on Rorke's Drift was a spontaneous action on the part of regiments disappointed at not having washed their spears at Isandhlwana. This was not the view of J. Y. Gibson, a magistrate in Zululand after the war, who talked with Cetewayo's brother, Undabuko. It is not unreasonable to suppose that Undabuko was to some degree in his brother's confidence, yet he, it seems, was not aware of any prohibition on crossing the Buffalo. Undabuko told Gibson that '. . . on seeing that portion of the army which had not been engaged cross the border, he called to members of his own regiment, the Mbonambi, to join them; but that they declined *on the ground that it was necessary to return to the field of battle to attend to their wounded*'.* It was not suggested that to cross the Buffalo would have been contrary to orders. Whatever the reason, it was fortunate indeed for the defenders of the Drift, already outnumbered by forty-five to one, that the Mbonambi turned back.

The inDlu-yengwe moved swiftly round the lower slopes of the Oscarberg to attack the post from the rear. Some of the uDloko and the uThulwana threw themselves at the hospital end. Here there was little cover, while the defenders, firing steadily from their loopholes, were largely hidden. Some of the warriors consequently moved to the cover of one of the ovens and cook-house opposite the commissariat store, or circled the eastern end of the post by the cattle kraal. Others returned to the main body of the *impi*, which was assaulting the long mealie-bag

* Author's italics.

wall on the north side. Here there was more cover: the patch of uncut bush; the five-foot-high stone wall which Witt had started but never finished; the ditch on the far side of the road, only thirty yards from the defenders; and the rock ledge itself, below the mealie bags. The whole area was a seething mass of yelling, frenzied Zulus, hundreds upon hundreds of them.

The range was close, and the British standing along the barricades were firing steadily into an enemy so numerous that they could scarcely miss. Sometimes the red-coats could not load and fire fast enough; then the warriors would be at the wall itself and the struggle became hand to hand, a welter of thrusting assegais and stabbing bayonets. Attack after attack was beaten back, the ground in front of the walls becoming increasingly covered with dead and dying Zulus. To add to the pressure on the defenders, some warriors armed with rifles had placed themselves on the terraces of the Oscarberg, from where they kept up a harassing fire. The soldiers at the back wall were comparatively safe, for the Zulu shooting was usually inaccurate, but from time to time one of the men at the front wall would drop with a bullet in his back.

All along the perimeter the battle ebbed and flowed. When beaten back, the warriors would crouch temporarily in whatever cover they could find, beating upon their shields with their assegais, and shouting in chorus. Then, reinspired, they would mass and hurl themselves on the wall, with a total disregard for their lives. They trampled over the bodies of their dead to grapple with the defenders at the bloodied wall of mealie bags. They seized the rifle muzzles and grabbed at the bayonets, to be spitted or blasted at point blank range, or clubbed down by a rifle butt when a soldier had no time to thrust a fresh cartridge into the breech. The noise was deafening: the incessant rifle fire; the clash of assegai on bayonet or rifle barrel; and the swelling chorus of the war-cry *uSuthu!* from 4,500 Zulus, reaching a fresh crescendo with each rush.

George Smith, the chaplain, moved continuously around the perimeter, administering words of encouragement to the men, and thrusting fresh ammunition into their hands or pouches from a large haversack he carried. Whenever his supply ran out, he replenished it from the boxes in the commissariat store. For his gallant conduct during the fight, he was later commissioned into the Army Chaplains Department and became widely known as 'Ammunition' Smith. Commissary Dalton, actively engaged in firing at the Zulus, was directing the men's fire wherever the attacks were fiercest. Suddenly he was hit in the shoulder, and Reynolds pulled him away to dress the wound. Corporals Schiess and Scammell, of the NNC, both on the sick-list, had dragged themselves from the hospital to assist in the defence. Scammell was hit and collapsed at the feet of L. A. Byrne, a twenty-two-year-old acting storekeeper. Hardly had he done so when Byrne, shot in the head, fell dead across him. Scammell, seeing Lieutenant Chard short of ammunition, pushed Byrne's body away and dragged himself across to give Chard his own ammunition. Schiess, with his bandaged leg, was at the mealie-bag wall when he was hit, again in the foot. Ignoring this fresh wound, the corporal mounted the barricade and bayoneted a Zulu who fired at him, knocking off his hat. He replaced it in time to shoot a second Zulu, who was followed so closely by a third that Schiess had no time to reload, and had to kill him with his bayonet.

The situation inside the hospital was even more desperate and it was here that some of the most heroic scenes of that day were enacted.

Several patients besides Scammell and Schiess had left the hospital to fight at the barricades. Of the remainder, only nine were totally incapacitated; the rest could at least fire a rifle from the loopholes hacked in the wall of their cell-like rooms. Before the Zulus came into sight, a number of soldiers had been detailed to barricade themselves into the hospital to assist in its defence.

The room at the front of the hospital building, with a door to the outside, contained five sick men, and was held by John Williams and Joseph Williams, two privates of the 2nd/24th. Private Horrigan, 1st/24th, who was ambulatory, assisted the two men in barricading the door and making loopholes. The corresponding room in the back of the building, which also had an exterior door, was defended by another patient, Private Waters. In the front corner room, to the right of the Williamses, two patients, Adams, a private of the 2nd/24th, and an artillery man named Howard, were also defending themselves. In the corner at the back of the building was a small room, occupied by the wounded Zulu patient, which had an outside door and an interior one connecting it with the next room. The outside door was barricaded by Henry Hook and Thomas Cole – 'Old King Cole', as he was inevitably known. The adjoining room was larger, and held nine patients. There were a further seven patients in the two small rooms on the other side of the one occupied by Waters, and these were defended by Private Robert Jones and Private William Jones. These two end rooms had a connecting door, and an outside exit, which was blocked with mealie bags.

Private Hook, a Gloucestershire man who had served in the Kaffir War of 1877–8, prided himself on his marksmanship, picking off several Zulus while they were still at a distance. For a while the black horde was held back from the rear walls by crossfire from the hospital and the storehouse. There was some accurate shooting from the rear wall itself: Private Dunbar, a friend of Hook's, killed nine warriors, one of them an *inDuna*, with nine shots. Soon the sheer weight of Zulu numbers began to tell; scores of them ran through the fire to the hospital itself, where they crouched against the wall, below the loopholes, or hurled themselves against the doors. They seized the soldiers' rifle barrels, trying to wrench them away or spoil the aim; they fired through the loopholes; they stabbed through the holes with their assegais.

The Zulus were swarming around us, and there was an extraordinary rattle as the bullets struck the biscuit-boxes, and queer thuds as they plumped into the bags of mealies. Then there was a whizz and rip of the assegais, the spears with which the Zulus did such terrible work . . .*

'Old King' Cole told Hook that he could stand it no longer, and dashed outside. He was killed instantly. Hook was left, with the moaning Zulu patient, as the sole defender of the two end rooms. Without Cole, he had two loopholes to defend: the Zulus began shooting through whichever one was unmanned.

A new dimension of horror was now added to the plight of

* Hook, H.

the hospital's inmates, some of whom were too badly injured to move: the Zulus set fire to the thatched roof. To stay meant being roasted alive; to venture outside was to invite the same fate as had befallen Cole.

The heat and the dense, choking smoke soon left Hook no option but to abandon the Zulu patient in the small end room and retire to the next one, through the frail communicating door. He did so only just in time, for the Zulus burst through the outer door and could be heard talking to their wounded comrade. They then assegaied him. Hook now found himself defending nine sick men, while the fire in the roof blazed even more fiercely.

Suddenly, two patients came through the other communicating door, closely followed by John Williams, crying, 'The Zulus are swarming all over the place! They've dragged Joseph Williams out and killed him!' The Williams's ordeal had been even more harrowing than Hook's. With the hospital in all probability soon to be cut off or abandoned, the roof on fire and the Zulus on the verge of breaking down the door, John Williams had begun, with a pick-axe, desperately to hack a hole in the wall separating their room from the next. Joseph Williams and Horrigan meanwhile concentrated on keeping their assailants away from the door. At last the hole was large enough for John Williams to crawl through and he started to drag the sick men after him. John had only time to rescue two before the door, which Joseph Williams had been bracing with his body, gave way. In the doorway, Joseph fought with desperate bravery, shooting or bayoneting all who approached. At last he was rushed, and his body, riddled with assegai wounds, was literally dismembered by the maddened warriors, who then butchered Horrigan and the other two patients.

Hook and John Williams now had eleven sick men to defend and their position was critical, for the Zulus could attack not only from the room which Hook had abandoned, but from the one from which Williams and his two charges had emerged. They were, as Hook put it, 'pinned like rats in a hole'. John Williams again went to work with his pick-axe, to gain access to the room defended by Waters. Hook defended the door from the corner room, shooting fast enough to keep the warriors back. A thrown assegai struck his helmet, and forced it back-wards, causing a scalp wound, but he fought on:

Only one man at a time could get in at the door. A big Zulu sprang forward and seized my rifle; but I tore it free and, slip-ping a cartridge in, I shot him point-blank. Time after time the Zulus gripped the muzzle and tried to tear the rifle from my grasp, and time after time I wrenched it back, because I had a better grip than they had.

All this time Williams was getting the sick through the hole into the next room – all except one, a soldier of the 24th named Conley, who could not move because of a broken leg. Watching for my chance, I dashed from the doorway and grabbing Conley I pulled him after me through the hole. His leg got broken again, but there was no help for it. As soon as we left the room the Zulus burst in with furious cries of disappointment and rage.

Now, with the heat and smoke from the burning roof increasing every moment, the whole harrowing process began all over again. With bullet and bayonet, Hook kept the Zulus away from the hole in the wall, while Waters manned the loophole. Williams was furiously hacking a third hole, which would lead them into the room occupied by the two Joneses and their patients. It took Williams, tired by now, some time to break through and enlarge the hole sufficiently, but finally he did so and the eleven patients were laboriously dragged through. At the last moment, Hook left his place by the hole in the other wall, and again succeeded in dragging Conley out after him.

William Jones and Robert Jones, aided by Corporal Allen and Private Hitch – both of whom refused to retire to the shelter of the perimeter despite being wounded – had managed to evacuate six patients to the veranda of the storehouse. Here they were tended by Reynolds, himself under fire. Sergeant Maxfield, still delirious, was left behind in the hospital.

By this time, Lieutenant Chard had been obliged to with-draw the men holding the north and south walls to the barrier of biscuit boxes which bisected the original defended area. The hospital was now thirty yards outside the perimeter, although firing from the storehouse area was keeping the gaps between the two buildings fairly clear of Zulus.

The prospect now before Hook, Williams and the others still

inside the hospital was formidable. This last room had a single window, six feet from the ground, and it was necessary to hand the patients up to the sill and then drop them down to Allen and Hitch outside. Incredibly, nine of the sick men staggered, crawled or were dragged across that terrible thirty-yard space between the buildings, amidst a hail of Zulu bullets and assegais. One, Trooper Hunter, a Natal Mounted Policeman, was not so lucky. He began to crawl across, being too sick to stand, and a Zulu sprang over the mealie bags and assegaied him. Hunter managed to kill his assailant before expiring, and their bodies were found together afterwards. When Robert Jones went back into the hospital to try to move Maxfield, he found he was too late: the Zulus were already in the room, and had stabbed the delirious sergeant to death. Waters decided against risking the dash in the open and, taking his chance with the fire, hid himself in a wardrobe. The two Joneses, Williams and Hook were the last to leave the fiercely burning hospital.

It was now some time after six o'clock, and the already intense pressure on the shortened perimeter began to increase as those warriors who had been storming the hospital came to support their comrades. In particular, they redoubled their efforts against the cattle kraal, where the walls were too low to afford the soldiers much protection. As darkness fell, the red-coats began to fall back to the wall dividing the kraal. Still the Zulus pressed on, in charge after charge, stepping over their own dead and dying, who lay thick on the kraal floor. Again, they could not be held back; sheer weight of numbers carried them howling through the soldiers' murderous fire to the hedge of bayonets, to fight it out hand to hand. At last, the soldiers were forced out of the kraal and all the survivors now stood within the main enclosure.

There was still a large heap of mealie bags in front of the commissariat store, and Chard ordered some of the men to pile these into a redoubt nearly eight feet high, with sufficient room in it for some of the wounded and a score of riflemen. This was to be the place for the final stand: from here there could be no retreat.

For hours, seemingly endless to the handful of defenders, the attacks came on, in a scene of carnage and fury illuminated by the flames from the still blazing hospital. The Zulus, pounding at the little fort like a black tide lashing a storm-wracked island, seemed without number, and with inexhaustible supplies of courage. They tried to set fire to the storehouse roof with brands tied to assegais, but soldiers on the roof threw them down. They hurled themselves time and again at the barricades. Most died before they reached it, but some succeeded in getting to grips with the defenders, and some even forced their way inside the enclosure. When there was no time to thrust a fresh cartridge into the breech, there followed desperate individual struggles with bayonet or rifle butt against shield and spear.

Sometimes, there would be a lull, while the Zulus performed a war-dance, to goad themselves to a new level of frenzy. And then, shouting their war-cry 'uSuthu!' on they would come again. At midnight, the battle was as fierce as ever. The chaplain was still going round issuing ammunition and Reynolds was busy patching up the wounded. The men, some of them so weary they could barely stand, were having trouble with their weapons. After continuous firing for eight hours, the barrels of the Martini-Henry rifles were becoming fouled. They grew so hot that they burned the soldiers' hands and, worse, caused the rolled brass cartridge-cases to soften in the breech, jamming the weapon. Henry Hook, for one, had several times to stop and clear his piece with the cleaning rod. Some of the long 'lung' bayonets, as the men called them, were beginning to twist and buckle from frequent and violent use. These were terrible weapons, which could transfix a Zulu and pin him to the ground. Thirst became such an acute problem that a small party of men, braving the Zulu horde lapping round the wall, fought their way to a water cart some distance outside the perimeter and dragged it to the wall of the enclosure.

At about 2am, the Zulus began to tire. Instead of repeatedly charging, they crouched behind the ovens, the cook-house, in the ditches, behind the walls of stone and mealie bags, even behind the piles of their own dead, continuing to harass the defenders by steady rifle fire and showers of assegais. This went on until, at about 4am, as the last flicker of flames from the gutted hospital died out, the shooting slackened and, little by little, ceased entirely. Quiet, strange to the ears of the troops after the incessant tumult of the past twelve hours, descended upon the night.

Chard dared not permit his exhausted men the rest they so desperately craved and so richly deserved. If the Zulus renewed their attack, and pressed it hard, the depleted garrison could hardly hope to withstand it. Of the original 104 able-bodied defenders, fifteen were now dead and two mortally wounded. Of the remainder, hardly a man was without a wound of some kind. Relief, moreover, seemed an unlikely prospect. Chelmsford's force had been twenty miles away from Rorke's Drift when the attack started, and could have moved only slowly during the night. Even if the general intended to make towards the Drift, the victorious *impi* might still be lurking to contest his passage.

As the eastern sky paled, and the hills of Zululand became visible, Chard, Bromhead and their men could see that their worst fears were not, for the moment, to be realised. The *impi* had vanished with the darkness. The only Zulus in sight were dead ones. They lay thick upon the ground, in piles, in rows, singly and by the dozen. By the mealie bags, around the ruined hospital, in and around the kraal, by Witt's unfinished wall, in the ditches, by the ovens, inside the first perimeter and out in the patch of uncut bush they lay, sprawled in every position of death, their cow-tail fringes and head-dresses bloodied and dusty. Amongst the bodies was strewn the litter of battle which the night had hidden. Assegais by the hundred, twisted and useless bayonets, broken rifles, oxhide shields and tattered bits of British uniforms. Everywhere, empty cartridge cases lay scattered like pebbles on a beach, more than 20,000 of them fired by the defenders.

When it was fully light, Chard ordered some of the men out to patrol the area and gather up all the weapons lying about. Hook went across to a soldier who was still looking over the barricade with his rifle at the ready, and spoke to him. The man did not reply, so Hook, thinking the man had fallen asleep, pushed his helmet back. There was a bullet hole in the fellow's forehead.

Not all the Zulus were dead. One seized Hook's leg as he walked by with an armful of assegais. Dropping the spears, Hook struck the man in the chest with his rifle butt, and then despatched him. After that, the men were ordered not to go about singly. Nearly 400 bodies were counted round the post, and the Zulus had taken a further hundred down to the drift. For days after the battle, dozens more were found on the Oscarberg and in the bush around the mission. The exact number of Zulu casualties will never be known.

The immediate concern of Chard and Bromhead was to ensure that the post was in as good a state of defence as possible. The barricades were repaired. Ropes were put through the hospital's loopholes and the walls pulled down, so that they should not provide the enemy with cover. The storehouse roof was torn off, to prevent the Zulus setting fire to the thatch should they attack again.

At about 7am, it looked as though the defences were again to be put to the test, for the *impi* suddenly reappeared on the western Oscarberg. The garrison stood-to, but the attack did not materialise. The Zulus were exhausted, and hundreds were wounded. They had been on the move since the previous Saturday when they had left Ulundi, and had not eaten for four days. The fighting at Rorke's Drift had tried their strength to the utmost, so after resting and taking snuff the *impi* rose, and Dabulamanzi led them away.

Shortly afterwards, to the intense relief of the garrison, Colonel Russell rode into the post with a force of mounted infantry, followed closely by Chelmsford and the rest of the survivors of the Central Column. They were greeted by roars of cheering from the defenders, who waved their tunics and helmets wildly. Chard made his report; and then Hook, to his acute embarrassment, was summoned, in shirtsleeves and braces, to give the general his account of the fight in the hospital, which was recorded by Captain Penn-Symons.

The dead were then buried: the Zulus in two large holes in front of the hospital and the British at the foot of the Oscarberg. Later, a memorial was erected, and a bandsman named Mellsop cut the lettering using broken bayonets as chisels.

Then, finally, the defenders of Rorke's Drift ate and slept.

To the secretary of state, Lord Chelmsford wrote of them:

The defeat of the Zulus at this post and the very heavy loss suffered by them has to a great extent neutralized the effects of the disaster of Isandhlwana, and it no doubt saved Natal from a serious invasion.

The cool determined courage displayed by the gallant garrison is beyond all praise and will I feel sure receive ample recognition.

It did. When Sir Garnet Wolseley arrived in South Africa to replace Chelmsford in June, he brought with him eleven Victoria Crosses for the defenders of Rorke's Drift. Chard and Bromhead, who were also promoted major, each received the decoration. The others were awarded to Privates Hook, John Williams, William and Robert Jones, Hitch, Corporal Allen, Surgeon-Major Reynolds, Commissary Dalton and Corporal Schiess. Neither before nor since have so many Victoria Crosses been awarded for a single action.

Chapter five
The Right Flank Column

Survivors of Isandhlwana began to stagger into Helpmakaar at sundown on the 22nd: there were about fifty colonials in addition to five imperial officers. Major Spalding, who had remained at Helpmakaar with two companies of the 1st/24th instead of returning with them to Rorke's Drift, now set about fortifying the town.

News of the disaster spread like wildfire across Natal, and the settlers all along the border prepared to face the horrors of a Zulu invasion. Pietermaritzburg was eighty miles away, and it was not until the evening of the 24th that two of Durnford's officers, Stafford and Newnham-Davis, rode in to confirm the rumours that had outstripped them on the road. The next day, Norris-Newman, the newspaper correspondent, arrived to give the colonists the first true picture of events at Isandhlwana, and of the casualties that had been sustained. The populace of Pietermaritzburg, and of Durban also, was in the grip of panic. Frere and Bulwer had no means of knowing that the great *impi* had dissolved and its warriors scattered to their kraals all over Zululand. Memories of the ravages of Dingane's *impis* were revived, and in Pietermaritzburg a great laager was formed, streets barricaded and walls loopholed in expectation of an imminent attack. Every male, from small boys to old men, was issued with a rifle and ammunition.

At Helpmakaar a court of inquiry to examine the causes of the disaster was instituted by Lord Chelmsford, but after hearing the testimony of the surviving officers it failed to come to any conclusion. Tired and dispirited, Chelmsford rode into Pietermaritzburg on Sunday, the 27th, and the same evening wrote a despatch to Hicks Beach, outlining what had befallen and expressing the hope that the court of inquiry would 'be able to collect sufficient evidence to explain what at present appears to me to be almost incomprehensible'.

Military activity on the part of the remnants of No 3 Column ground to a halt, pending the arrival of reinforcements. Life was miserable enough for them; sickness was rife, they had lost most of their equipment, and possessed only the clothes they stood up in. The immediate prospect was gloomy indeed. Two of the NNC regiments deserted and some colonial volunteers dispersed to their homes. The panic in Natal spread into the Orange Free State, while in the Transvaal the restless Boers seemed disposed to seize the British setback as an opportunity to reassert their independence.

Lord Chelmsford's conscience with regard to Isandhlwana was clear: he had left unequivocal orders to defend the camp and a force strong enough to do so. Yet, as he waited in enforced inactivity for reactions and reinforcements from England, the horror of the disaster which had overtaken his command ate deeper and deeper into his mind. Finally, on 9 February, his exhaustion, depression and frustration compounding one another, he wrote a letter to Colonel the Honourable F. A. Stanley, Secretary of State for War, which contained the following passage:

I consider it my duty to lay before you my opinion that it is very desirable, in view of future contingencies, that an officer of the rank of Major-General* should be sent out to South Africa without delay.

In June 1878 I mentioned privately to His Royal Highness the Field-Marshal Commander-in-Chief, that the strain of prolonged anxiety, physical and mental, was even then telling on me. What I felt then, I feel still more now.

This letter was a request for assistance rather than an offer of resignation; a request for a second in command to share some of the burden of administration and succeed him if the need arose. But the press and the public at home, unable to decide whether to pin the blame for the disaster on Chelmsford or

* Chelmsford, a major-general, held the local rank of lieutenant-general.

Durnford, seized upon the letter, which had the unfortunate effect of intensifying the outcry.

News of Isandhlwana did not reach England till 11 February, when it was taken late that night to Hicks Beach at his house in Portman Square. It marked, though he probably did not realise it at that moment, the end of the confederation policy. For Disraeli, already ill, the shock was so great that he took to his bed. The public, the cabinet, the opposition, the newspapers, the army, were all galvanised. Until this moment the South African situation had been quite eclipsed by the war in Afghanistan with its overtones of a possible imbroglio with Russia. The country was accustomed to reports of administrative successes and military victories. Defeat, especially so crushing a defeat at the hands of savages, was intolerable, and by his very victory, Cetewayo had ensured his ultimate destruction. So, while the commander-in-chief telegraphed to Lord Chelmsford that he was 'satisfied that you have done and will continue to do everything that is right', arrangements were put in hand to send reinforcements to South Africa in far greater numbers than Chelmsford had requested, or had started the campaign with in the first place.

Five infantry regiments, each over 900 strong, were marshalled in England: the 94th Regiment; the Rutlandshire Regiment; the 3rd Battalion, the King's Royal Rifles (the 60th); the 2nd Battalion, Royal Scots Fusiliers; and Princess Louise's Argyllshire Highlanders. From Ceylon, the 57th Regiment was ordered to Zululand. Two regular cavalry regiments, the 17th Lancers and the King's Dragoon Guards, each with 622 men and 480 horses, were ordered to prepare for embarkation. Two field batteries of artillery were assembled, plus drafts for the Royal Artillery units already in South Africa. There were, in addition to the fighting units, three companies of the Army Service Corps, with horses, mules and wagons, and a unit of the Army Hospital Corps. All these – together with a gathering of newspaper correspondents, notably F. Francis of *The Times*, Archibald Forbes of the *Daily News* (who was at the time on the North-West Frontier in India), and Melton Prior of the *Illustrated London News* – converged on Southampton and Portsmouth, and by the end of February had set sail for the theatre of war.

It will be recalled that Chelmsford's plan for the invasion of Zululand involved three columns. Besides the Central (No 3) Column, now *hors de combat*, Colonel Evelyn Wood commanded the Left Flank (No 4) Column, and Colonel Charles Pearson the Right Flank (No 1) Column.

Around the earthern fort, called appropriately Fort Pearson, on the Natal side of the Lower Drift, the Right Flank Column had assembled ready for crossing the Tugela River into Zululand. It was a strong force, the nucleus of which was formed by the five companies of the 2nd/3rd Regiment, the Buffs – Pearson's own regiment – and the 99th Regiment under Lieutenant-Colonel W. Welman, plus a detachment of the Royal Artillery with two guns. The Naval Brigade had provided 200 bluejackets from HMS *Active*, who had brought two 7-pounders with them, and a Gatling gun. Major Barrow of the 19th Hussars led a force of over 300 mounted men, drawn from a number of volunteer colonial units. Besides a company of Royal Engineers under the command of Captain Wynne, there was a half company of the Natal Native Pioneer Corps, and two battalions of the 2nd Natal Native Contingent, led by Major Graves and Captain Beddoes respectively. In order to move this force, 3,500 oxen and other transport animals had been assembled, and 384 wagons looked after by 620 civilian wagon conductors. In all, Pearson commanded some 2,500 men.

Early on the morning of 12 January (ten days before the Isandhlwana disaster), the Right Flank Column started crossing the Lower Drift by means of a punt attached to a hawser and pulled by teams of oxen. Most of the column was across by late on Monday, the 13th, and while mounted patrols scoured the country ahead for signs of Zulu activity – without, however, finding any – the rest of the force set to work to construct a second fort, named Tenedos after a cruiser lying offshore. The fort would command the Lower Drift, which when the Tugela began to fall would be easily forded by an *impi*, thus exposing the coastal area, and Durban in particular, to some danger.

Pearson's plan was straightforward. Leaving two companies

1 Sir Henry Bartle Edward Frere, Governor of Cape Colony and High
Commissioner in South Africa

2 Cetewayo, King of the Zulus

3 Lieutenant-General Lord Chelmsford, KCB, commander of the
South African Field Force

4 The survivors of Isandhlwana crossing the Buffalo at Fugitives' Drift

5 The cavalry revisiting the field of Isandhlwana to bring away the wagons

6 Russell's horsemen reach Rorke's Drift the morning after the battle. On the left is the cattle kraal, and next to it the commissariat store with the final redoubt of mealie bags in front. Behind the trees are the wagons in the rear wall. To the right, the still burning shell of the hospital

7 The battle of Gingihlovu: Barrow's horsemen pursue the retreating Zulus

8 Inside the square at Ulundi. Lord Chelmsford and his staff are seen mounted, right of centre. The picture gives some idea of the activity during a battle: wounded men and animals, stretcher bearers and surgeons, ammunition carriers, closely packed transport and waiting cavalry

of the 99th, part of the NNC and some of the sailors to hold
Fort Pearson and Fort Tenedos, and so control the crossing, he
proposed to move the rest of his force, in two parts, thirty-seven
miles into Zululand, to Eshowe. From the mission station there
he would be in a position to co-operate with the Central
Column under Glyn and Chelmsford.

Accordingly, shortly after first light on the 18th, Pearson
marched out of Fort Tenedos with part of the Buffs, half the
mounted men, the Naval Brigade, the pioneers and the 1st/2nd
NNC. Progress was slow. Heavy rain had reduced the track to
mud and swollen the streams it was necessary to cross. The first
eight miles lay through open grassland, but thereafter the ground
began to rise, and was thickly covered with bush. The Inyoni
River proved a difficult obstacle to the wagons, and in the afternoon Pearson's force camped twelve miles from their starting
point.

The four companies of the 99th, which were to accompany the
column, the rest of the mounted men and the 2nd/2nd NNC left
Fort Tenedos on the morning of the 19th under the command of
Lieutenant-Colonel Welman, reaching the camp on the far side
of the Inyoni before Pearson's men had pushed on. By that
evening, Pearson's part of the force, and most of Welman's men
as well, had advanced another four miles across a stream called
the Umsundisi, but the wagons were delayed at the Inyoni.
Ahead lay another, larger river, the Amatikulu, which was
known to have a difficult drift. Pearson decided to remain where
he was for a day in order to give the wagons time to catch up,
and Wynne's engineers and the native pioneers a chance to make
the drift more passable. The advance continued on the 21st.

On the 22nd – the day of Isandhlwana – the column pushed
slowly on, the mounted troops scouting the thick bush, and the
pioneers doing what they could to facilitate the passage of the
wagons. After crossing the next stream, the Inyezane, Pearson
halted the column for breakfast. The leading wagons drew up,
and while the rest continued to cross the Inyezane, the men
spread out on either side of the track to eat.

The meal, however, was interrupted. The track ahead rose
over the shoulder of Majia's Hill, along the crest of which some
Zulus appeared. Pearson sent Lieutenant Hart's NNC company

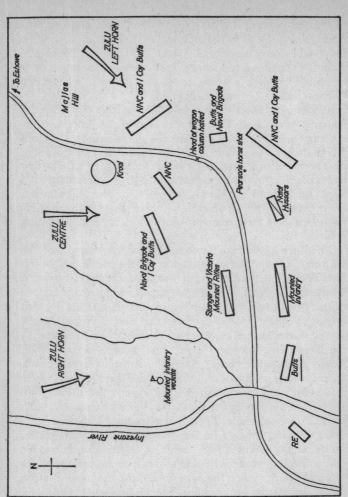

5 The battle of Inyezane

to evict them. Hart's men proceeded up the track, but the Zulus retired to the east, and Hart, nothing loath, went after them, only to find himself confronted with a force much larger than he had expected: charging towards him were some 6,000 warriors. These, the men of an *impi* five regiments strong, had been sent to Majia's Hill to fall upon Pearson's column as it was strung out at the Inyezane drift. Hart's natives had sprung the trap prematurely.

The NNC company, seeing the overwhelming force of Zulus bearing down upon them and being armed with very few rifles, fled towards the track along which they had advanced, leaving their officers and NCOs to fire into the oncoming *impi*, already throwing out its horns as it raced down the hill.

Pearson sent some of the Naval Brigade and two companies of the Buffs doubling up the track to establish themselves on a knoll to the right of the track where they were joined by the two artillery pieces in opening a destructive fire on the Zulu left horn. A few of the warriors made good practice in reply. One in particular shot very accurately and the best of the troops failed to silence him, until one of them climbed a tree and shot him from there. The Zulu centre, meanwhile, had swept rapidly into a deserted kraal on the side of the track, opposite the knoll and 400 yards from it. The two guns were now turned in this direction. To their fire was added that of the Naval Brigade's Gatling gun* which some of the bluejackets under the command of Midshipman Cadwalader Coker had manhandled into position.

The engineers working on the drift joined Major Barrow, who had dismounted his horsemen, and, reinforced by some of the Buffs, they brought the right horn of the *impi* to a standstill. The Zulu attack was being held, but the position was hazardous. Pearson's horse was shot from under him. His force had been caught in open order, in country covered with much dense bush. The wagons, spread out along the track and across the drift,

---

* The Gatling gun was used for the first time by the British Army in Zululand. Invented by an American in 1862, it was a multi-barrelled weapon made in a variety of calibres and capable of firing upwards of 800 rounds a minute. The cartridges were fed into the action from a hopper on top of the gun, which was mounted like a small field gun on a wheeled carriage.

were particularly vulnerable. Fire from the British infantry and guns was heavy, however, and the Zulus had few firearms between them.

Under cover of the field guns and the Gatling, Commander Campbell and 100 men of the Naval Brigade, supported by a company of the Buffs, stormed the kraal, drove the Zulus out of it and set fire to the huts. This move effectively knocked the centre out of the Zulu line.

Barrow and his force started to roll up the Zulu right, and by 9.30am the *impi* had fallen back over Majia's Hill. So ended the battle of Inyezane. The Zulus took their wounded with them, but were estimated to have suffered 300 casualties. Sixteen of Pearson's men were wounded, and the ten dead were buried on the spot in a grave dug by the engineers.

The column reached Eshowe the following morning. The mission, now deserted, consisted of a brick church with a tin roof, a school building and a house situated in a grove of orange trees. A stream ran past the church. Tents were pitched around the mission, and the troops at once began to dig shelter trenches. On the 25th, the men, under the direction of Captain Wynne and his engineers, started the construction of a regular fort, 200yds long and 50yds wide, right round the camp. The earth thrown up from the moat, which itself was to be 20ft wide and 7ft deep, was formed into a solid wall 6ft high. Pearson intended that it should be thoroughly Zulu-proof. Four dozen empty wagons were sent back for supplies to Fort Pearson with an escort of two companies of the 2nd/3rd and two of the 99th.

On the evening of the 26th, Colonel Pearson received the first news that all was not well with the Central Column, in the shape of a note from Sir Bartle Frere at Pietermaritzburg. The message was confusing rather than informative, for it announced only that Durnford was dead and his natives defeated. There was no amplification of this until the 28th, when a runner arrived at Eshowe with a telegram from Lord Chelmsford, also now at Pietermaritzburg:

The unfortunate disaster which has occurred to No. 3 Column has I fear placed you in a very awkward position, as the indirect support which we were able to give you has of course ceased to exist. I do not see any prospect of being able to push forward either No 3 or No 4 Columns until reinforcements come out from England ... My hope is that the Zulus will soon try and knock their heads against your entrenchments and that you will then be able to give them the lesson they require ...

Chelmsford's telegram went on to say that all previous instructions to Pearson were cancelled, and that he was to act entirely upon his own initiative. He should withdraw from Eshowe if he considered his position too exposed, or he could construct an inner redoubt that could be held by only a fraction of his force if he sent the rest back to Natal. The only things the telegram made quite clear were that Pearson could expect to have the entire Zulu army down upon him, and that he could expect no assistance. It was not a helpful message. A major reverse of some sort had obviously occurred, but precisely what, Pearson was left to speculate upon. The news of Isandhlwana filtered through only slowly in the following weeks.

Pearson discussed the column's predicament with his officers, who recommended withdrawal. But the arrival of the loaded supply wagons – seventy-two, more than he had sent back – caused a change of heart, and it was decided to hold Eshowe with a reduced force.

Accordingly, on 28 January, Major Barrow left the camp with most of the mounted volunteers and the Natal Native Contingent. Although the country between them and the Tugela River was by now swarming with hostile warriors, Fort Tenedos was reached without incident.

Pearson withdrew his 1,300 soldiers and bluejackets, and the wagon conductors, into the now completed fort at Eshowe, where they camped beneath the wagons parked behind the walls. The Zulus began to close in. They captured a herd of 600 draught oxen which Pearson was sending back to Fort Tenedos with an NNC escort to reduce the forage problem; in so doing they ensured that Pearson remained where he was, since the loss of the oxen made it impossible to move the wagons.

On 6 February a runner got through to Eshowe with another letter from Lord Chelmsford, in which he asked Pearson to hold out for as long as his supplies permitted, expressing the hope that the garrison would be able to fight a successful action before retiring. Two days later, however, the general wrote:

My last information tends to show that the Zulus will avoid knocking their heads against Ekowe, [sic] and that their intention is to raid in force into Natal.

If this be true it is more important than ever that you should be on the Tugela with a movable force. . . .

It would not be surprising if Pearson was confused by such contradictory instructions. He had already written to Chelmsford expressing worry over the responsibility of holding or not holding Eshowe. He looked for a directive, but found none. Unwilling to commit himself irrevocably to either course of action, he wrote to the general that he would retire from Eshowe in mid-February with the 99th, the Naval Brigade and half the engineers, enabling the remainder of the garrison to eke out the food and ammunition a while longer. The message, however, failed to reach the Tugela.

The defenders, under Captain Wynne's energetic supervision, continued to strengthen the fort against the massive force which was always expected, but never materialised. The dry moat was filled with sharpened stakes, and the ground provided with distance markers to make sighting more accurate. These the Zulus pulled up under cover of darkness, until deterred by means of improvised mines. The mounted men who were left pushed patrols out into the surrounding country and skirmished with parties of warriors. The remaining oxen were driven out of the fort each morning to graze, protected by one of the infantry companies. There was bathing in the stream, with separate pools for officers and men.

Despite a reduction in the rations, food was adequate, though monotonous. Heavy rain fell frequently, and many of the men, sleeping on the ground beneath the wagons, began to fall ill. Dysentery set in, and soon the church – which Norbury, the naval surgeon, had taken over as a hospital – was full, while his medical supplies dwindled. He attempted to obtain fresh supplies by native runners, but was reduced in the end to improvisation.

Pearson had discovered that seven miles away to the north was a kraal owned by Dabulamanzi, Cetewayo's brother, and this he determined to attack. Early in the morning of 1 March, the colonel led 400 men out of the fort and reached the kraal at

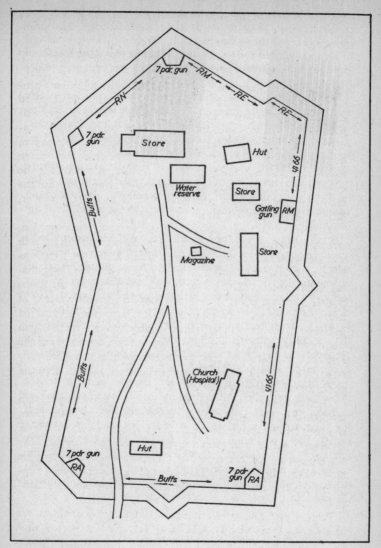

6 The fort at Eshowe

first light. Most of the inhabitants fled before Pearson's men could come up, but a few opened ineffectual rifle fire. The kraal was shelled and set on fire. Pearson withdrew. The episode was of no account, but it doubtless served to improve the morale of the troops whose chief enemy by this time was boredom rather than Zulus.

The next day an event occurred which was far more important and exciting for the garrison. A heliograph was seen flashing from Fort Pearson, over thirty miles away. After several days of frustration, when clouds obscured the sun and interrupted transmissions, it was at last learned that on the 13th a column was setting out to relieve Eshowe and that the garrison was to sally out and meet it on the Inyezane. On the 6th, much to the intense disappointment of the men at Eshowe, the heliograph announced that the relieving column could not march until the beginning of April.

By this time, one of the officers at the fort had improvised a crude heliograph out of a piece of metal tube and a pocket mirror, and two-way communication was possible. After all official messages had been passed, time was allowed for private traffic. Pearson, whose wife was due to give birth, flashed: 'How is Mrs Pearson?' 'Mrs Pearson is . . .' came the reply from the Lower Drift; then the clouds interrupted, and the colonel was left for hours suspended on tenterhooks, waiting for the sun to reappear. Then the heliograph flashed again, '. . . well and delivered of a baby daughter'.

As March wore tediously on, the Eshowe garrison waited impatiently for relief. All the tea and coffee were soon used up and the men were reduced to slaughtering the draught oxen for their stringy meat. Luxuries were few and far between, rapidly rising to a price that few could afford. A tin of sardines fetched 11s, and a bottle of pickles 1s more. A box of matches realised 4s, and the price of tobacco rose to £1 per lb. The number of sick increased. By the end of the siege, 120 men were ill, and four officers and twenty-one men were dead.

Chapter six
The Left Flank Column

With the remnants of the Central Column back in Natal and unable to take the offensive for the time being, and Pearson's column invested at Eshowe, only Colonel Evelyn Wood's Left Flank (No 4) Column remained active.

Wood's force was 2,086 men strong. The backbone of the column was formed by two imperial infantry battalions, the 1st/13th Regiment, commanded by Lieutenant-Colonel Gilbert, and the 90th, led by Lieutenant-Colonel Cherry. These were supported by 110 men and a battery of six 7-pounder guns of the Royal Artillery, under Major Tremlett, and there were also a few Royal Engineers. Wood was particularly fortunate in having Colonel Redvers Buller to lead a very strong force of more than 700 mounted men, drawn from a variety of units, mostly irregular colonials,* of which the Frontier Light Horse was the largest single group, and including a small force of volunteer Dutch, led by Piet Uys.

Wood had crossed the Blood River on 10 January, and established a camp at Bemba's Kop; from there, on the 18th, he moved in the direction of the White Umfolozi, two days' march away. Here he camped near the kraal of a chieftain named Tinta, who decided to make his peace with the British and was sent back to Utrecht under the watchful eye of a company of the 90th.

While the rest of the force set about erecting a stone laager on the southern bank of the White Umfolozi, Buller immediately set out with some of his horsemen on a reconnaissance towards the table-topped Zunguin Mountain, thirteen miles to the north, known to be harbouring a substantial number of Zulus. Their

* Mounted Infantry, Frontier Light Horse, Transvaal Rangers, Baker's Horse, Kaffrarian Rifles, Dutch Burghers, Border Horse, Mounted Basutos, Wood's Irregulars.

reaction to this intrusion was immediate and vigorous: an *impi* of 1,000 warriors attacked Buller's men, who were obliged to fall back almost to the river before shaking off the Zulus.

Wood, hearing of this, determined to take the counter-offensive forthwith, and at midnight on the 21st he marched his column – except for a single company from each of the infantry battalions left to garrison the camp – to join Buller, who did not return to camp that night. The mounted men pushed on to reach Buller's small force as quickly as possible, while the 90th and the 1st/13th followed at their best pace.

Reunited again, Buller and Wood began to climb Zunguin while it was still dark, leaving Lieutenant-Colonel Gilbert and the 90th below on the plain at the southern end of the mountain. By first light, the British force was at the summit and the Zulus, finding themselves confronted with far more powerful opposition than on the previous afternoon, departed rapidly along the table-top and across the nek which connected Zunguin with the next mountain in the range – Hlobane, massive, flat-topped, and with precipitous sides.

Wood's men marched along the Zunguin plateau, from the northern edge of which they could see, moving about on the top of Hlobane, a force of Zulus estimated at 4,000. It was evident that the mountain, a great natural stronghold firmly held by the Zulus, would have sooner or later to be reduced before the northern end of Zululand and the Disputed Territories could be subdued.

The exertions of the day had been strenuous, so Wood decided to spend the 23rd in camp on the plain below Zunguin. Early next morning the column set out to try to come to grips with the *impi* on Hlobane. As the troops approached the hill, three or four thousand Zulus were seen above, some of whom opened fire on the British. A few shells from the 7-pounders dispersed them, but there was nearly a misfortune. As the Zulus departed, the 90th Regiment marched rapidly off to try to intercept them, leaving their wagons unguarded. Seeing this, several hundred warriors poured down the mountain towards them and, but for the timely arrival of Buller and the Frontier Light Horse and Uys' Boers, they would have been destroyed.

As the skirmish petered out, a Kaffir arrived with a note from

Captain Gardiner, telling Wood the news of Isandhlwana. He immediately marched his men back to the camp at Tinta's kraal. It was evident to him that the collapse of No 3 column meant that a temporary break in the invasion of Zululand was certain. It was equally evident that, as his own force could not advance on Ulundi alone, it was now out on a limb – deep in Zululand without any means of support. Tinta's kraal had been chosen only as a temporary camp, a supply depot; not being supplied with firewood, it was unsuitable as a permanent base. Wood decided to move to Kambula Hill, on the Blood River, twenty-two miles east of Utrecht and fifteen from Hlobane, taking with him as much of the supplies that had accumulated at Tinta's kraal as he could find transport to carry.

The column reached Kambula on 31 January and set about establishing an entrenched and fortified laager in a strong defensive position on the hill. Wood received a letter from Lord Chelmsford giving him, like Pearson, complete freedom of action – which suited Wood exactly – and warning him that he might soon feel the weight of the entire Zulu army. 'I must trust to you and Pearson to re-establish our prestige,' wrote the general. 'My best thanks are due to you and Buller. I feel confident that you two are going to pull me out of my difficulties.' Then, with a fine disregard for the parlous situation in Zululand and Natal, Chelmsford turned to a personal matter: 'I was horrified when I heard that there was talk of giving you a CMG. I had written before to the Duke of Cambridge and I wrote again when I heard it to say that the *least* reward you were entitled to was a KCMG.'

Wood, however, was not much concerned about such things for the present, and wrote back to that effect; for, despite chronically bad health, he was determined that his column should not sit idly on the defensive. In Colonel Redvers Buller, 'a silent, saturnine, blood-thirsty man,' as Archibald Forbes* called him, he possessed an ideal lieutenant; a brilliant leader of irregular horse, tough, fearless, resolute, untiring, who ruled his motley command with a rod of iron. This, indeed, was as well, for these horsemen were a mixed bunch, consisting of 'broken gentlemen, of runagate sailors, of fugitives from justice, of the

* Forbes, A. *Barracks, Bivouacs and Battles.*

scum of the South African towns, of stolid Africanders . . . there were a few Americans . . . a Greaser; a Chilian; several Australians; and a couple of Canadian voyageurs from somewhere in the Arctic regions.'* Predictably, these volunteers lacked the smartness of regular units. They dressed as they liked, mostly in brown breeches and jackets, and a slouch hat. They were armed with Martini-Henry carbines and revolvers, and about the only uniform item of their equipment was their ammunition bandoliers.

The day after the column reached Kambula, Buller led the mounted men off to attack a military kraal at Makulusini, thirty miles away in a depression surrounded by precipitous hills. Arriving at noon, Buller, leaving thirty men to protect his line of retreat, dispensed with all precautions and galloped into the kraal with the rest of the force. There were 250 huts in all, which were rapidly set on fire. Only about 100 Zulus were present and these fled without making much resistance. Six of them were killed. Buller's men retired, driving 270 head of cattle before them.

Buller was relentless. He raided to the west; he raided northwards in the country beyond the Black Umfolozi; on 10 February he struck at the kraals around Hlobane and captured another 500 head of cattle. He rested his various troops of horsemen, but never seemed to rest himself. He would ride all day, every day, fifty miles and more. His horse, a 'fiddle-headed, brindled, flat-sided, ewe-necked cob' named Punch, was remarkable for his ugliness, outstanding strength and endurance. He could go 100 miles at a stretch and was, moreover, a 'salt' horse, proof against horse-sickness. Buller seemed never to be off his back and, when he was, slept fully dressed.

The camp on Kambula Hill proved unsatisfactory. It was a long way from the nearest timber supply, and frequent rain combined with the fact that neither the Boers nor the Natal Kaffirs could be persuaded to use the latrines had rendered the ground insanitary. In mid-February Wood decided to move to a new site two miles away along the ridge. Here, on a tongue of elevated ground, he formed a seven-sided wagon laager and 100 yards to the east, on slightly higher ground, a long narrow re-

* Forbes, A. *Barracks, Bivouacs and Battles.*

doubt big enough to hold a couple of infantry companies. Between and to the front of the laager and the redoubt, a cattle kraal was established, connected to the redoubt by a palisade of stakes. The guns were placed in the open, between the laager and redoubt, and the Kaffirs were given quarters in some huts three or four hundred yards to the east. The wagons in the laager were run close together, the *disselboom* of each under the one in front of it, and the wheels were lashed together in order to make it virtually impossible to overturn any individual wagon. Trenches were dug around the outside of the position, and the earth from them thrown up into parapets. It continued to rain.

In the middle of March a fresh disaster struck Chelmsford's Field Force.

The main road by which military supplies were passed between the Transvaal and Natal ran up from Luneberg – garrisoned by five companies of the 80th Regiment, under Major Charles Tucker – through Derby to Middleburg, 130 miles away. Five miles beyond Luneberg, the road crossed the Intombi River, a tributary of the Pongola, at Myer's Drift. The road, being close to the Zulu border, was frequently raided.

Towards the end of February, a convoy of wagons left Lydenburg in the Transvaal laden with supplies for Natal. On 1 March, Major Tucker sent 'D' Company of the 80th out to escort the convoy into Luneberg, then changed his mind; recalling 'D' Company, he sent another, under the command of Captain David Moriarty. This company reached Myer's Drift on the Intombi on 7 March, to find seven of the wagons on the north side of the stream, heavy rain having swollen the river too much to permit the convoy to cross. Of the rest of the wagons there was no sign.

Moriarty now displayed a degree of resourcefulness, managing to find enough materials to construct a raft; on this he had by the following morning ferried seventy of his 103 men across. Then, leaving one of his two lieutenants, Harward, with the men on the southern side of the river, and a few others to pitch camp on his side, Moriarty marched off in the direction of Derby to try to locate the missing wagons.

By the 9th, the convoy was reassembled at Myer's Drift,

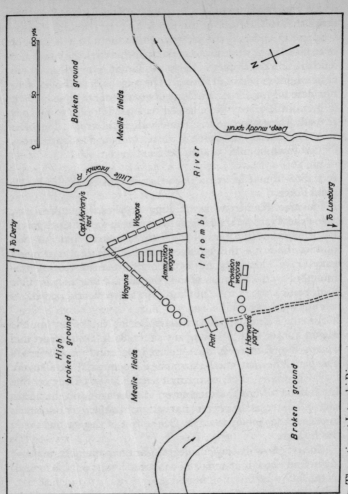

7 The action at Intombi River

which was still impassable. There was nothing for it but to make camp and wait for the river to go down.

Moriarty arranged the wagons astride the road in the shape of an inverted V, the legs not quite resting on the river bank. The left leg ended in a row of four tents. The wagons were not run close together, and no real attempt was made to make the position defensible. The ammunition wagons were parked inside the laager, but Moriarty had his own tent pitched *outside* the apex of the V. On the south bank, Harward's platoon had set up their three bell tents in a neat row, with their two wagons beside them.

The Intombi failed to subside, and the convoy and its escort of the 80th were still camped on the drift when Major Tucker rode out from Luneberg on the afternoon of the 11th. He pointed out that Moriarty's wagons were too far apart and that his position should have been resting on the river, but Moriarty, who expected to be able to cross next day, made no alteration to his arrangements. After all, the Zulus were unlikely to attack a position only five miles from Luneberg, which was strongly garrisoned. That night, in flat contradiction to the orders promulgated by Lord Chelmsford to the Field Force, only a single sentry was posted on either side of the Intombi, and no pickets were thrown out at all.

At about 4am, while it was still dark, the sentry on the southern bank was alerted by a single shot on the far side, and Harward's men stood-to. Apparently, nobody on Moriarty's side heard the shot; at any rate, nobody on the north side stirred.

About an hour later, as the first light enabled the men on the south bank to see the wagons on the far side, a tremendous volley of shots broke out from a position upstream of Moriarty's encampment, followed immediately by the charge of a Zulu force about 1,000 strong. Harward's men opened fire and the Zulus' reaction was swift: several hundred of them turned and dashed straight into the fast flowing river, to attack the men on the southern bank.

Moriarty himself put up a gallant resistance, but most of the troops and wagon conductors stood no chance; they were speared within a few moments as they tumbled out of their tents and wagons.

One of the wagoners, Josiah Sussens, who survived, left an

account of his harrowing experiences. He was asleep in his wagon and woke to find the laager swarming with Zulus, busy assegaiing everyone in sight. In the confusion of the moment, Sussens couldn't find his rifle, and bolted towards the river clad only in his shirt. As he did so, he heard Moriarty shout, 'Fire away men; I am done!'* There were other men in the river, and those Zulus with rifles were shooting vigorously at any heads they saw. Whether deliberately or by accident, Sussens lost his shirt, but by swimming most of the way under the water, he reached the southern bank. This too was seething with warriors, engaged in trying to wipe out Harward's party, and Sussens recorded that '. . . in my desperation I contemplated throwing myself in the water to be drowned peaceably' rather than face the Zulus' assegais. On second thoughts, he resolved to try to reach Luneberg.

Harward, though more alert than Moriarty, had still no time to organise his small force cohesively, and the fight rapidly dissolved into struggles between isolated groups, or individual redcoats and overwhelming numbers of warriors. Lieutenant Harward then mounted his horse and galloped off in the direction of Luneberg. This, he afterwards maintained, was to fetch help, he being the only mounted man.

A small group of soldiers led by Colour Sergeant Booth, who possessed more presence of mind than his commander, fell back slowly. The men had begun the fight with seventy rounds each, and by carefully directed volleys the Zulus were held at bay for three miles. The still naked Sussens managed to join this group, and one of the soldiers gave him a coat. Booth still had his little band together – though somewhat depleted – when Major Tucker arrived with reinforcements. The Zulus then retired. For his gallant conduct in conducting this withdrawal, Booth was later awarded the Victoria Cross.

The Intombi River affair had cost the lives of sixty-two men of all ranks, plus fifteen Kaffirs, two of the wagon conductors and Cobbin, the civilian surgeon, who was with the company. Failure to laager properly and underestimation of the fighting qualities of the Zulus caused the disaster at Myer's Drift just as at Isandhlwana, which can hardly have made the news any

* Wilmot, A. *History of the Zulu War.*

more palatable to Lord Chelmsford. What upset the general as much as these further unnecessary casualties was the fact that Harward had left his men. Moriarty, who bore direct responsibility for the disaster, had paid for his carelessness with his life, and Chelmsford was reluctant to voice criticism of a dead man, as he had been in the case of Durnford.

Harward was court-martialled. There were two charges against him. First, he had 'misbehaved', a euphemism for having displayed cowardice in leaving his men at a moment of extreme danger. Secondly, he had failed to take proper precautions for the safety of his men. The first charge was legitimate enough. The second suggests that Harward was to be made a convenient scapegoat in place of Moriarty. It was he, not Harward, who should have insisted that the camps were picketed correctly, and if the camp on the south side of the river was not in a proper state of defence, Moriarty should have ordered Harward to make the necessary alterations. In the event, Harward was acquitted on both charges and released to return to his duties.

In London, Sir Garnet Wolseley, reviewing the verdict of the court, was disgusted. He could not interfere with the decision, but he could withhold his approval and confirmation. He did so in the following terms:

Had I released this officer without making any remarks upon the verdict in question, it would have been a tacit acknowledgement that I concurred in what appears to me a monstrous theory, viz., that a regimental officer who is the only officer present with a party of soldiers actually and seriously engaged with the enemy, can, under any pretext whatever, be justified in deserting them and abandoning them to their fate. The more helpless the position in which an officer finds his men, the more it is his bounden duty to stay and share their fortune, whether for good or ill. It is because the British officer has always done so that he occupies the position in which he is held in the estimation of the world, and that he possesses the influence he does in the ranks of our army. The soldier has learned to feel that, come what may, he can in the direst moment of danger look with implicit faith to his officer, knowing that he will never desert him under any possible circumstances.

It is to this faith of the British soldier in his officers that we owe most of the gallant deeds recorded in our military annals;

and it is because the verdict of this Court-Martial strikes at the root of this faith, that I feel it necessary to mark officially my emphatic dissent from the theory upon which the verdict has been founded.

For once Wolseley and the Duke of Cambridge were in complete agreement. The commander-in-chief acquiesced in Wolseley's order, and by his command it was read at the head of every regiment in the army.

Chapter seven
Hlobane and Kambula

Towards the end of March, Lord Chelmsford, having received reinforcements from England, was almost ready to march to the relief of Pearson. He wrote to Wood asking him to stage a diversion in the area of Kambula to lure away the *impi* that Cetewayo was said to have sent to mask Eshowe.

Ever since the skirmish at Zunguin, the Zulu stronghold on Hlobane had been much on Wood's mind. The warriors there had been reinforced by others from Ulundi and, when the time came for Wood to resume the advance into Zululand, he would not be able to leave so formidable a position in his rear. In a letter to Chelmsford on 3 March, Wood had expressed the fear that it might cost him half a battalion to take the mountain; but by the 12th he was more optimistic and wrote to the general, saying he was now considering assaulting the stronghold.

To do so would undoubtedly provide the diversion requested by Chelmsford, but Wood's sudden change of mind suggests that the project was ill-considered, and out of character for so experienced and wily a fighter. It was indeed a risky undertaking: nobody had any idea, except what could be seen from the plain below, of the physical obstacles to climbing up on to the plateau. To make things more difficult, it was decided to commence the climb in the dark, so as to surprise the Zulus. The mounted volunteers rather than the infantry were to make the assault, presumably because of the distance of Hlobane from the camp. Wood had received reliable information that a powerful *impi* was marching from Ulundi, on the 26th or 27th, to attack him and, if possible, to repeat the victory of Isandhlwana. Nevertheless, on 26 March, Wood issued his orders for the attempt, writing the same day to Chelmsford, 'I am not VERY sanguine of success.' It is difficult to understand Wood's motives for undertaking such an operation, which by his own account had a poor chance of success.

Hlobane consists of an elevated plateau about three miles long, largely encircled by precipitous cliffs, and connected at either end to lower plateaux running in the same east-west direction. The easternmost plateau was joined to Hlobane by a saddle known as Ityenka Nek, and the whole feature was an extension of Zunguin Mountain.

To compensate as far as possible for the lack of topographical information, Wood determined to assault Hlobane from both ends at once. While Buller led the main force up the eastern end of the mountain, Colonel Russell would take a smaller force and demonstrate at the western end.

Buller's horsemen, nearly 400 of them, were in the saddle before dawn on the 27th, having been issued with three days' rations and a double allowance of ammunition, a fact which suggested to the men that this was to be more than a mere reconnaissance. Captain Barton led 156 men of the Frontier Light Horse; Piet Uys brought thirty-two of his Boers, and there were seventy-one Transvaal Rangers under Commandant Raaf. Baker's Horse fielded seventy-nine men under Lieutenant Wilson. Major Tremlett commanded a seven-man rocket party. Lieutenant-Colonel Weatherley and his fifty-three men of the Border Horse were late in starting, and 277 Kaffirs of Wood's Irregulars brought up the rear on foot.

By early afternoon Buller's men had reached a position to the south of Zunguin, where they off-saddled for a meal. As they passed the cliffs on the southern side of the mountain, a few shots were fired at them, but without effect. At sunset, the men bivouacked at a deserted kraal south of Ityenka Nek, lit fires and ate again. Buller, with his instinct for irregular warfare, had no intention of being caught in his camp, or of betraying his movements. After the moon had set, the men saddled up, and throwing plenty of wood on their fires, moved off in the darkness to the foot of Hlobane. From ten o'clock that night until 3.30am on the 28th, the troopers got what sleep they could, resting on the stony ground, with the horses ready saddled.

At half-past three, Buller began the ascent of Hlobane. It was a difficult task in the darkness, and a thick mist made it doubly

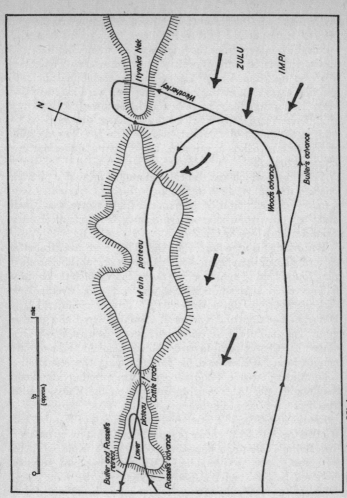

8 The action at Hlobane

so. After a while the ground became so precipitous that the men had to dismount and lead their horses. It was hard to distinguish the boulders from the grass between them, and men and beasts floundered as they groped their way upwards. The horses plunged and slipped, some falling back on the animals behind, pinning them against the rocks; a number were killed in this way. After a time the wind rose, and the mist was replaced by a thunderstorm; lightning helped to illuminate the way up. To add to the men's discomfort, torrential rain followed; soon everyone was soaked to the skin, and the going underfoot was churned to mud.

First light, which saw the column almost on to the plateau, enabled the Zulus to see their danger. Firing broke out. Lieutenant von Stietencron, of the Frontier Light Horse, was killed, and so were two troopers. Lieutenant Williams received a wound from which he died.

Reforming his tired horsemen, Buller led them away from the eastern edge of the plateau, while numbers of Zulus began slipping round behind him, blocking the track by which the column had ascended. It was now impossible to retire via Ityenka Nek without fighting. Buller ordered 'A' Troop, Frontier Light Horse, to dismount and hold a ridge running across the plateau to prevent the Zulus from harassing his rear. With several of his officers, he then rode off towards the western end of the mountain to locate Russell and his force, leaving the rest of the column to follow and Wood's Irregulars to round up any cattle they could find. 'A' Troop opened fire on the Zulus, whose numbers were increasing every moment.

Lieutenant-Colonel Russell had marched out of Kambula at 1pm on the 27th with a force of 640. Though not much smaller than Buller's column, it was composed largely of Kaffirs. There were 240 of the 1st Battalion of Wood's Irregulars, seventy mounted Basutos under Captain Cochrane of the 32nd Regiment, many of whom had fought at Isandhlwana, and 200 Zulus whose chief had submitted to Wood's protection. Commandant Schermbrucker led forty Kaffrarian Rifles. There was a small rocket party led by Lieutenant Arthur Bigge, RA, and eighty mounted infantrymen, commanded by Captain Browne, 1st/24th. On the night of the 27th, Russell's force bivouacked five miles to the east of Hlobane.

Wood and his staff, with an escort of six Zulus and eight men of the 90th, left Kambula at about three in the afternoon and spent the night with Russell's column.

Russell started his force up Zunguin Nek at the western end of Hlobane some time after Buller and his men had commenced their scramble at the other end. The climb was steep and the men had to lead their mounts; but there was no opposition, and by dawn they were on the lower plateau. Russell pressed forward to examine the track leading up on to the main plateau. It was, he discovered, a steep, rocky cattle path across a razor-backed ridge barely passable for horses. He sent Captain Browne up the main plateau to find Buller and assess the situation. Browne later returned, having been unable to contact Buller, who, he thought, had ridden back to find Wood. He had spoken to Major Tremlett and Major Leet, who were trying to discover a way down the western end of the mountain passable for horses.

Wood, meanwhile, had ridden along the southern side of Hlobane towards Ityenka Nek, with the intention of following and joining Buller, but without knowing that the Zulus on the top were already closing the eastern track. Near Ityenka, Wood met Weatherley, who had started late from Kambula with the Border Horse and had been unable to locate Buller in the dark and the storm. Buller's whereabouts were almost immediately disclosed, however: the crackling of rifle shots could be heard high above on the plateau, as the fire of the Zulu snipers was returned.

Bidding Weatherley and his men to follow, Wood at once started to ascend the track, guided by the sound of shooting, and by the dead and injured horses which marked the path. By now it was light, enabling Wood to see the formidable nature of the mountain up which the main force had struggled in the darkness and rain.

Wood and his staff, either fitter or more adventurous, soon outpaced Weatherley, and as they neared the rim of the plateau came under fire from both front and flanks. Mr L. H. Lloyd, the political officer, was mortally hit. Wood and Captain the Honourable R. Campbell, his chief staff officer, pulled Lloyd back out of fire, where he died. Directing the Border Horse to brush the Zulus aside, Wood started upwards again, leading his horse, which was immediately shot and killed.

Weatherley's men, who by now had lost five killed and six or seven wounded, were showing marked reluctance to get to grips with the enemy; so Campbell, taking with him Lieutenant Lysons, the orderly officer, and three or four of the 90th from Wood's escort, dashed up the track towards the cave from which the most telling fire was being directed. Campbell was hit in the head and died instantly. Nothing daunted, Lysons charged into the mouth of the cave, driving the Zulu marksmen deep inside it. Weatherley and his men, shamed into action, now came up.

Campbell's body was taken back down the track. He had been a close friend of Wood's. Mindful perhaps of the mutilation of any dead bodies found by the Zulus, Wood resolved to bury Campbell and Lloyd then and there on the mountainside, notwithstanding the fact that his men were hotly engaged with the enemy. Sending a bugler back through the heavy fire to retrieve a prayer-book, which belonged to Campbell's wife, from the saddlebag of his dead horse, Wood hoisted the two bodies on to the back of another horse and took them down the mountainside away from the firing. There he set the six Zulus of his escort to dig a grave with their assegais, and when the bodies had been buried, Wood calmly read the burial service from the prayer-book.

By the time this had been done, Weatherley's men had reached the plateau, now abandoned by 'A' Troop, and disappeared from view. Wood decided to retrace his steps and ride back to the western end of Hlobane, to see how Russell's force was faring and await the arrival of Buller. As Wood made his way down the flank of the mountain, the view out across the plain to his left was blocked by a fold in the ground. One of his Zulus, riding along the top of this ridge, suddenly called to Wood and waved. Lloyd had been the only officer present able to speak Zulu, so Wood, unable to understand, rode up the rise to see what was the matter.

The sight before him must have taken his breath: below on the plain, about three miles away, was the great *impi* reported to be marching on Kambula from Ulundi: over 20,000 warriors in five huge columns, masses of black relieved by the colour of the warriors' shields and by the sun glinting on their assegais. The main body of the *impi* was moving in the direction of Kambula, and was already parallel with Hlobane. As Wood watched, the right horn of the army detached itself, making towards the western end of the mountain. Their intention was clear: to trap the soldiers on the plateau. Hundreds of warriors were breaking away from the rear of the great *impi* and coming towards Ityenka Nek, to cut off any retreat.

As Wood could not tell whether Buller and Russell had seen the *impi*, he sent Lysons, his sole remaining staff officer, to Russell with a message: 'There is a large army coming this way from the south, get into position on Zunguin Nek.'

Wood then followed, with two thoughts in his mind. Buller and Russell must be got off the mountain before they were trapped; and the whole force must reach the camp at Kambula before the *impi*. It was now about 10.30am.

Russell had, in fact, seen the approaching *impi* an hour and a half earlier, and had despatched a messenger to inform Wood. The track over the razorbacked ridge connecting the upper and lower plateaux was so bad that Russell had decided it was impracticable to take his men up to support Buller in the event of a retirement to the east. Leaving a few men at the nek, he had taken the rest of his force back down on to the plain. Here he met Lysons with Wood's message. Russell was not very familiar with the ground and, misinterpreting the order, led his men five miles away to the west, where they played no further part in the day's action.

On the flat top of Hlobane, meanwhile, desperate events had been taking place.

'A' Troop of the Frontier Light Horse, which Buller had left as rearguard at the top of the eastern track, were soon under heavy pressure from Zulus on their front and flanks. Buller reached the nek at the western end of the plateau, after Captain Browne had left it, and deciding, like Russell, that it was passable only on foot, he resolved to send his Kaffirs down by it and return to the eastern end with the mounted men. Buller then sent Captain Barton, of the Coldstream Guards, with a party of thirty men from the Frontier Light Horse, to ride ahead and bury the officers and men who had been killed in the ascent.

When Barton, his face blackened by a powder discharge, reached 'A' Troop's position, he found them barely holding their ground, but ordered them to do so at all costs. They held on for a while, until the Zulus, in overwhelming numbers, surged forward, 'all yelling like fiends out of hell'. 'A' Troop retired precipitately, but the Zulus were quickly amongst them, their spears flashing in all directions. A seventeen-year-old trooper, 'Chops' Mossop, was stabbed in the arm, but shot his assailant dead. The Zulu force was already throwing out its horns behind the troopers, with a line of warriors forming across the plateau, barring the retreat. Luckily Mossop's Basuto pony, Warrior, was still fresh and very agile; putting him straight at the line, Mossop rode two Zulus down and made his escape, to ride on westwards in search of the rest of the column.*

By this time Buller had seen the approaching *impi*, and realised that he had no chance of descending via Ityenka Nek. It would have to be the western nek, however impassable it looked. He sent two men galloping after Barton, with an order to abandon the burial and 'retreat at once to the camp by the right side of the mountain'. When he issued this instruction, Buller was presumably facing east, the direction in which Barton had gone, and his right would therefore have been the south. That is clearly not what he intended, since it was from the south that the great *impi* was swiftly approaching. When Barton received the order he must have been facing the same way, and retired to the south unaware of the danger.

He soon discovered his error. Caught with Hlobane behind him and the *impi*, hardly half a mile away, spread out across his front, Barton – who had been joined by Weatherley and his men – had no option but to retreat across the Ityenka Nek. The Zulus who had earlier detached themselves from the main *impi* were there before them, however. In desperation, the small body of colonial horsemen charged into the press of warriors. Sixty-six of the eighty-three men were quickly surrounded and assegaied.

Weatherley died heroically. He succeeded in cutting his way through with his sabre, but his fourteen-year-old son, who had

* Mossop, G. *Running the Gauntlet.*

been riding with the Border Horse, was trapped. Weatherley rode back into the mass of Zulus to get him, and tried to mount the boy behind a trooper. But the lad refused to leave his father, who pulled him up into his own saddle. Father and son died together.

Barton got through and gallantly took an unhorsed man up behind him. The two rode for several miles, relentlessly pursued by a party of warriors who at last came up with them. The man he had saved was shot and Barton surrounded. His revolver misfired three times, and he was then shot and speared to death. The story of his end was later recounted by a warrior named Tshitshili, who after the war guided Colonel Wood to the spot.

The rest of Buller's column meanwhile reached the western extremity of the plateau, where their position was critical in the extreme. It was a nightmare scene. The sides of the plateau, which fell sheer away, converged on the nek down which the cattle track ran to the lower plateau, forming a funnel into which Buller's men were tightly jammed. There was no longer any semblance of order and units were hopelessly mixed up. There was no organised rear-guard to hold off the Zulus, who had now swept along the plateau and were pouring a heavy fire into the British ranks.

Worst of all, the cattle track in front of them, which Buller had earlier pronounced impassable, dropped almost perpendicularly for 120 feet, in a series of rocky steps. Some of these, only inches wide, were three, four or even five feet apart, and on either side the ground fell away steeply. The Kaffirs, panic-stricken, were already swarming down it. Few of them reached Kambula.

Young 'Chops' Mossop, viewing the chaos, asked a trooper next to him if there was any chance of getting through, for to add to the horror the Zulus were already busy with their assegais. 'Not a hope!' said the man, and, sticking the muzzle of his carbine into his mouth, blew out his brains, which splattered all over Mossop. The young trooper dismounted and started to fight his way down the nek on foot. Slipping amongst the boulders and the bodies of men and horses, Mossop suddenly felt a vice-like grip on his shoulder and a terrific blow on his ear. It was Buller. 'Where is your horse?' demanded the colonel.

'Go back and get him. Don't leave him again.' To this stern command Mossop undoubtedly owed his life.

Remounting Warrior at the top of the nek, Mossop tried to make his way down the cliff itself, but the pony, sure-footed though he was, slipped and his rider was thrown, dazed, into a crevice. Before Mossop could extricate himself, the body of a dead horse fell on him, pinning him in the hole, so that he had to squirm from underneath the carcass. Minus his hat and carbine, and bleeding from the stab wound in his arm, Mossop found Warrior; incredibly, the pony appeared to have only minor injuries, but the saddle-tree was broken and a stirrup iron missing. Mossop folded his jacket and placed it under the damaged saddle to protect the horse's back, then remounted and made his way to the bottom.

Others were having similar experiences. Captain D'Arcy, of the Frontier Light Horse, having seen all the men of his troop down the nek, followed amidst heavy enemy fire. Suddenly, a boulder 'about the size of a small piano' came crashing down on him. Somebody yelled a warning, but the rock tore off one of his horse's legs. Continuing on foot, D'Arcy was knocked down by a horse and rider, and almost crushed. He reached the bottom and started off at a run, but laden down with riding boots, field-glasses, a carbine, a revolver and seventy rounds of ammunition he was no match for the athletic Zulus. By great good fortune a trooper named Francis caught him a horse, but D'Arcy was no sooner up than he gave the animal to a man of the Frontier Light Horse who was wounded in the leg. D'Arcy then started running again, but Buller took him up and carried him to safety.

Buller was everywhere. Time and again he rode back to rescue men who had lost their horses in the descent or who were badly wounded. For his gallant conduct at Hlobane, he was awarded the Victoria Cross.

The *impi* on the plain had by now skirted the southern side of the mountain and reached the western end. The only line of retreat was to the north, and those men, exhausted, wounded or injured, who had a horse to ride, streamed away in that direction, while the Zulus finished off the not so fortunate.

Mossop and his pony reached a stream, and he dismounted to

drink; but, though the water refreshed him, exhaustion and loss of blood had so sapped his strength that he could not remount: his legs refused to move. The Zulus were getting closer, and in sheer desperation he finally managed to stand. As he pulled himself into the saddle, it slipped so that the coat fell off and the broken tree dug deep into Warrior's back. After getting clear of the Zulus once more, Mossop replaced the coat with his shirt and, partly walking, partly riding, reached Kambula that evening.

The great *impi*, tired by the march from Ulundi, bivouacked by Zunguin. The surviving horsemen limped into Kambula singly or in small groups till late into the night, heavy rain adding to their miseries. Buller, despite having been in the saddle for almost two days with virtually no rest, left the camp with fresh horses almost as soon as he reached it, and rescued at least seven more of the survivors.

While Lord Chelmsford had given Wood complete freedom of action when he asked for a diversion to cover the relief of Eshowe, the appearance of the *impi* at Hlobane had shown that the attack on the mountain had been as unnecessary as it had been ill-judged. Wood's column had nothing to show for the action but an appalling casualty list. Fifteen officers and seventy-nine men were dead, and eight seriously wounded. The casualties amongst Wood's Irregulars were impossible to assess; the unit had ceased to exist. Out of fifty-three NCOs and men, the Border Horse had lost thirty-nine dead; their survivors, like those of the Frontier Light Horse, were now seriously handicapped due to the number of horses killed or wounded.

On the night of the 28th, as the exhausted men of the Left Flank Column settled down to get what sleep they could in the rain, they did not even have the satisfaction of knowing that their casualties had been sacrificed to good purpose.

There was a curious sequel to the action at Hlobane. Amongst the troopers of Weatherley's Border Horse was a Frenchman named Grandier. During the retreat across Ityenka Nek, Grandier, near the tail of the column, mounted a wounded man on his horse, and was running alongside when a warrior seized him by the leg. For some reason the Zulus did not kill him at once, but took him to the kraal of Umbelini, on the southern side of Hlobane, where he was tied to a tree.

The following day, Grandier was dragged into the midst of the great *impi*, where his life was threatened, but an *inDuna* named Inzanane interrupted the proceedings, saying that the white man should be sent to Cetewayo. A day later, Grandier was entrusted to four mounted warriors for the four-day journey. The Frenchman, quite naked, was obliged to walk the whole way, carrying the food for the party.

On arrival at Ulundi, Grandier was left in the open, naked and bound. He was taken before the Zulu king at noon the next day, when with a Dutch-speaking half-caste as interpreter, Cetewayo demanded of him why the British were attacking him, and vowed revenge against Shepstone and everyone else. He then showed the Frenchman two guns, both spiked – presumably the ones taken at Isandhlwana – and a Portuguese who was engaged upon manufacturing guns for the warriors. Many Martini-Henry rifles were in evidence, as well as some English newspapers.

For ten days Grandier was kept prisoner at the royal kraal, fed only on mealies and frequently beaten. Then messengers arrived with news of the fight at Kambula and Umbelini's death there. Cetewayo decided to send Grandier back to Umbelini's people, so that they could have the pleasure of killing him. This time only two warriors were sent as escort. and at noon one day both of them lay down to sleep. Grandier seized an assegai and killed one, who was armed with a gun, and the other made off. For several days Grandier travelled on in the direction of Kambula, sometimes moving at night to avoid Zulu patrols. He was picked up by a mounted patrol on 15 April.

Although the veracity of Grandier's extraordinary story was questioned after the war, it earned him some renown at the time. He may certainly have embroidered the truth, but the fact remains that he was the only member of the Field Force taken prisoner by the Zulus or, at least, to survive the experience.

The rain departed with the night, and 29 March dawned clear and sunny. Wood must have known that the *impi* would assuredly come on and try conclusions at Kambula. This was confirmed quite early in the morning by the arrival of a friendly Zulu, who had fallen in with the warriors of the *impi* during the night and learned that they intended to attack Kambula at noon. This intelligence was useful to Wood, as the camp was running out of firewood, and consequently out of bread. Deciding to take a chance, he despatched two companies of the 1st/13th to cut wood on the slopes of Ngaba Ka Hawane, a mountain some five miles away, judging that they could be back before the attack developed. He also sent out Commandant Raaf with some of the Transvaal Rangers to locate the *impi*.

The otherwise peaceful morning was disturbed by the desertion of the Dutch Burghers; Piet Uys's death on Hlobane seems to have demoralised the Boers. Perhaps interpreting their departure as a bad omen, the surviving Kaffirs, always fearful of the Zulus, also decamped. The rest of the men occupied themselves in strengthening the laager. The rem-chains of the wagons were drawn taut and locked together beneath the wagon beds, making it all but impossible to overturn them. Plentiful supplies of ammunition were distributed, with reserves on hand.

At about 11 am the *impi* appeared to the east, and moved towards Kambula at a leisurely pace. It was in five great columns, composed of nine regiments, numbering more than 22,000 men. The firewood gatherers returned quickly to the camp. Having drilled his men to such a state of readiness that the tents could be struck and the defences manned in less than a minute and a half, Wood coolly insisted that the men should eat their dinner before standing-to.

By one o'clock all was ready, and the defenders of Kambula waited for the Zulu onslaught. The north, north-west and north-east faces of the seven-sided wagon laager were manned by the 90th Regiment, the others by the 1st/13th. The long, narrow redoubt to the east of the laager was occupied by a company and a half of the 90th, with two mule guns. Another company of the 1st/13th held the cattle kraal. The four field guns were in position between the laager and the redoubt.

As the *impi* approached the camp, it split, the left horn encircling the south of it, while the right horn worked around the northern perimeter, still out of range, and then halted. Eager to precipitate the attack, Wood ordered Buller and Russell out

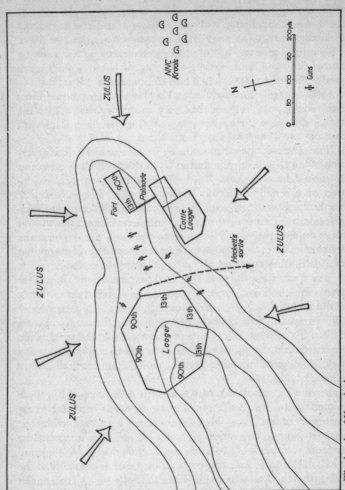

9 The battle of Kambula

with some of the mounted men. The horsemen rode to within 100 yards of the black horde, dismounted, and fired a volley. The effect was instantaneous: the 11,000 or so warriors of the right wing sprang forward with a tremendous shout. Inside the camps the tents were immediately struck, and Buller's men sprang into their saddles and galloped back to the laager.

Some of them were in difficulties. 'Chops' Mossop had been given a huge, ugly horse to replace Warrior, who had died from his injuries. The animal – 'a mountain of bones' – was so tall that Mossop could barely touch the stirrup-iron with his toe. When he attempted to remount, the horse refused to stand still and dragged Mossop, clinging desperately to the double bridle, in leaps and bounds, and at full gallop, with the Zulus in full cry after him. Seeing his predicament, Captain Oldham gallantly turned back and, by riding in front of the horse, slowed him sufficiently to allow Mossop to scramble into the saddle. The two men then galloped back to the laager, as the artillery opened fire over their heads. Not all the men were so lucky. Between the *impi* and the laager was a patch of swampy ground, which slowed down three of the riders, enabling the Zulus to overtake them and spear them to death.

The warriors came on, undeterred by the casualties caused by rifle fire from within the laager. It was a windless day, and soon the British perimeter was under a thick pall of smoke from the black powder cartridges. The men could see only a few yards and, under cover of this smokescreen, the Zulus came right up to them. There was a tremendous crash as the wall of shields struck the wagons. Some of the warriors started to force their way between and beneath the wagons. Mossop, busy firing through a hole slashed in the canvas of Piet Uys's old wagon, heard a shout of, 'They are in! They are in!' A company of the 1st/13th ran up and ejected the Zulus with fixed bayonets.

The smoke became so thick that the riflemen were by now firing blind and a bugle sounded the 'Cease Fire'. As the smoke lifted, the men could see the ground in front of the wagons thickly scattered with dead warriors. Some were lying amongst the wagons, others inside the laager itself. There was a pause, and then the *impi*, a vast black wall, came on again, the guns cutting them down in droves.

Wood, who had stationed himself on the ridge between the laager and the redoubt, behind the guns, was not averse to participating in the action himself. Private Fowler, one of his personal escort, had been trying to shoot a particular *inDuna* for several minutes, but without success. He said to the colonel, 'Would you kindly take a shot at the Chief, sir?' Wood took Fowler's carbine, put it to his shoulder, but discharged it prematurely, while still aiming at the Zulu's feet. The *inDuna* fell, hit in the stomach. Wood promptly potted two others by aiming low, before handing the carbine back to be sighted correctly.

The cattle kraal, held by a single company of the 1st/13th, now came under heavy attack, particularly from some of the Zulu marksmen who were making exceptionally good practice. Owing to the slope of the land, the ground beyond the kraal was 'dead', giving the warriors cover from the firing up on the ridge. After a while, the fight for the kraal, conducted amidst a couple of thousand trek oxen, became so fierce that at 2.15pm Wood decided to withdraw the company to the redoubt. As they fell back along the palisade, a soldier fell hit by a bullet. With characteristic gallantry and disregard for his position, Wood dashed forward to help him. Captain Maude, of the 1st/90th, prevented him and, with Lieutenant Lysons and Lieutenant Smith, brought the man in under heavy fire. Smith was hit, though not mortally.

Such acts of bravery and determination occurred all over the camp. Sergeant Allen sustained a bad wound in his arm, had it dressed, and was told to lie down in the improvised casualty station. Instead, he went straight back to the firing line, where he was promptly killed directing his men. When the cattle kraal was evacuated, Private Grosvenor, of the 1st/13th, stayed behind to look after Sergeant Fisher, who was badly wounded, and paid with his life for this selfless act. Captain Lethridge, who was in the hospital when the battle started, left his bed and, recklessly exposing himself, cheered on his men from a chair.

The Zulus were giving battle with the same courage and determination. Some of them, armed with Martini-Henrys taken at Isandhlwana, were maintaining a particularly galling fire from the long grass which had sprung up on the manure heaps by the horse lines. The company in the cattle kraal had suffered heavily from this before they were withdrawn. Wood sent a message to Major P. H. Hackett, of the 90th, who was in the wagon laager, asking him to make a thrust down the slope in front of the camp, and drive the Zulus back.

Accompanied by Captain Woodgate, 4th Regiment, who was acting staff officer to Wood, Hackett brought two companies of the 90th out of the laager, fixed bayonets, and charged down the slope. Before this onslaught, the Zulus retired, despite their numerical superiority. On reaching the bottom of the incline, the two companies halted and Hackett led them back towards the laager. The Zulus interpreting this as a retreat, immediately opened a heavy and telling fire. Lieutenant Bright, commanding 'G' Company, was hit in the thigh and died later in the day. Hackett was struck in the head by a bullet which blinded but did not kill him.

As the two infantry companies returned to the laager, the Zulus swarmed to the attack again, and the battle settled down into a pattern. The *impi* charged heroically up towards the British perimeter, to be met by withering rifle and artillery fire. They fell back, and then, sustained by the hope of achieving a second Isandhlwana – several of the regiments present had fought there – they came on again. At one point, the warriors pressed their attack so fiercely that they came to within 100 yards of the four guns in the open, commanded by Lieutenants Bigge and Slade, whose crews sent the horses inside the laager and continued to serve their pieces throughout the action.

Thus the fight continued for another three hours, until about 5pm. Then the Zulus, who had had no food for three days, and were weary and dispirited by their losses, began to withdraw. At half-past five Wood ordered the cattle kraal to be reoccupied, and shortly afterwards sent the mounted men out to harry the retreating *impi*. Somebody heard him mutter, 'I would willingly give £1,000 to have the Dragoons and Lancers here now.' He need not have worried: the irregular horsemen did their work thoroughly. The Zulus were pursued for seven miles, until it was too dark to see. Many were shot down. Commandant Scherm-brucker's Kaffrarian Rifles, not content to shoot, seized assegais from dead warriors and with these they stabbed and hacked in hand-to-hand combat.

The battle of Kambula was a decisive victory for Wood. It avenged, though it could not erase, the recollection of Hlobane. Three officers died of their wounds, eighteen men and NCOs were killed, and sixty-five of all ranks were wounded. The line battalions had expended on average only thirty-three rounds of ammunition per man; the artillery had fired 326 shells and eighty-six rounds of canister. Within 300 yards of the laager, 785 Zulus were collected for burial, but no estimate of those killed in the pursuit, or who died of their wounds, could be formed.

Isandhlwana had been a great victory for the Zulu army, though won at terrible cost. The price exacted for their failure at Kambula was equally fearful. Against hammer blows like these, not even the great-hearted courage of Cetewayo's *impis* could prevail, and another such blow was about to fall.

Chapter eight
The Relief of Eshowe

While Wood and Buller were busy raiding and fighting in the north, Lord Chelmsford had been gathering together sufficient strength to march to the relief of Pearson and his column at Eshowe. Following the news of Isandhlwana, reinforcements poured into South Africa as fast as ships could carry them. All through March they came, and by the 18th Chelmsford had assembled his relief force on the Zulu side of the Lower Drift of the Tugela, still flooded by torrential rain.

The column, under Chelmsford's personal command, was divided into two brigades. Lieutenant-Colonel Francis Law, RA, commanded the 1st Brigade, made up of the 91st Highlanders under Major Bruce; two companies of the Buffs and five of the 99th, both commanded by Major Walker, 99th Regiment; and 350 sailors of the Naval Brigade from HMS *Shah* and *Boadicea*. The 1st Brigade's artillery consisted of two 9-pounder field guns, two 24-pounder rocket tubes and a Gatling gun. In addition, there were 800 Kaffirs of the 4th Battalion, NNC, led by Captain Barton of the 7th Regiment, and men from the commissariat, transport and medical departments.

The 2nd Brigade, commanded by Lieutenant-Colonel Pemberton, 60th Rifles, was composed of the 57th Foot, under Lieutenant-Colonel Clarke, sent from Ceylon; six companies of the 60th Rifles, under Lieutenant-Colonel Northey; 290 sailors and marines, and the 5th Battalion, NNC. This brigade had two rocket tubes and one Gatling. There were also members of the commissariat, transport and medical staff.

In addition to the two brigades, Major Percy Barrow, 19th Hussars, commanded a force of divisional troops, comprising the native foot scouts, 150 mounted infantry and volunteers, and 130 mounted Kaffirs. The column's total strength was 5,670, of whom 3,390 were white. Chelmsford now had a stronger force than the original Central Column.

The general was well aware that Pearson could not hold out much longer and, in order to speed up his march as much as possible, baggage was cut to the minimum. No tents were to be taken, each man being allotted only a blanket and a waterproof sheet. Even so, the supplies for the column, plus extra for the garrison at Eshowe, required no fewer than forty-four carts and 100 ox wagons. Such a mass of transport would be strung out over two miles or more on the track. Chelmsford doubted whether he could advance more than eleven miles a day, since the oxen had to be frequently rested, especially in hot weather.

The transport situation caused Chelmsford some misgivings, and on 25 March he had sent a despatch to the secretary of state in which he expressed the hope that the inevitable slowness of the advance would be attributed to this cause, and not to any other. He also expressed his expectation of being attacked en route; and then he added, in words which show to what extent the Isandhlwana disaster had undermined his self-confidence, '. . . I trust that, should our efforts fall short of what is, no doubt, expected of us, circumstances may be duly taken into consideration'.

The words do not do justice to the general's determination that on this occasion there should be no slip-ups. The lessons of 22 January had not gone unmarked, and Chelmsford wrote in his own hand extensive and detailed instructions as to how the division should march, and how it should camp. Nothing was to be left to chance.

Companies were to march in close order, and files were never to be extended. Every cart and wagon in the convoy was to have ammunition readily accessible within it; the box-lids of the regimental reserves were to be unscrewed, and every wagon was to have a screwdriver. At night a square laager would be formed, surrounded by a shelter trench 9ft from the wagons. The Europeans would sleep between the trench and the wagons; the Kaffirs and animals inside the laager. The men were to be under arms at 4am each day, ready to march as soon as the scouts reported the vicinity clear of the enemy. No bugle calls except the alarm were to be sounded. At night, combined pickets of six white and six native troops were to be stationed half a mile in front of each side of the laager, and native scouts were to be thrown out a mile. In the event of the pickets falling back before an attack, special care was enjoined not to fire upon them.

The relief column marched at 6am on 29 March, following a route somewhat to the east of that taken by Pearson. The first day took the column to the Inyoni, and the second to the Amatikulu, which was flooded. On the 31st the troops struggled across the river, through water up to their chests, and on 1 April pushed on to within a mile of the Inyezane, the last natural obstacle before Eshowe. Chelmsford sited the laager for that night upon rising ground, devoid of any cover except long grass. It was 600 yards west of a stream called Gingihlovo, near the site of a kraal of the same name, which means, 'He who swallowed the elephant,' given by Cetewayo in honour of an early victory of his.

The march so far had been uneventful, but Major Barrow's mounted patrols, and John Dunn, whose scouts were accompanying the division, reported that the Zulus were concentrating, thus confirming Chelmsford's expectation that they would contest his passage to Eshowe. The nightmare possibility that the Zulus would attack while his troops and wagons were strung out on the track was a constant threat.

Chelmsford decided to remain where he was on 2 April, partly in the hope that the onslaught would take place while he was in laager, but also to rest the men and oxen, and give the ground time to dry. After a sodden night the day dawned mercifully fine; a white mist hung about the laager, suggesting a hot day to follow. Shortly before 6am the mounted men who had been out at daybreak came in with the news that the *impi* was approaching, and shortly afterwards the pickets opened fire and began to retire. Why the Zulus chose to attack an entrenched camp rather than wait for the column to be strung out on the line of march was inexplicable. Had they waited until the oxen were driven out to graze, they could, by capturing or driving them off, have immobilised the column. Chelmsford, however, was doubtless delighted: this was precisely the sort of battle he wanted.

The troops stood-to, and as the mist began to rise the *impi* came into sight across the Inyezane. There were about 10,000 warriors, of six regiments, all of which had been at Isandhlwana – the Ngobamakosi, the uVe, the umCityu, the umHlanga, the

Mbonambi and the uThulwana led by Dabulamanzi, who now commanded the *impi* as he had done at Rorke's Drift on 22 January. As the black mass approached the river, their regiments had already assumed their classic formation. The left horn splashed through the Inyezane and moved towards the northern side of the laager. The chest and right horn crossed further to the west, and approached the British position from the west and south.

Within the laager an air of expectancy prevailed. Only a few orders were given: 'Stand to your arms – saddle up – no independent firing – volleys by companies when they are within three hundred yards.' The suspense was too great for the petty officer in charge of the Gatling gun at the left front angle of the laager, who implored Captain E. H. Buller to let him open fire on a body of Zulus now only half a mile away. 'Beg your pardon, sir,' he said, 'last night I stepped the distance to that bush where those blacks are, and it's just eight hundred yards. This "no firing" seems like throwing a chance away. I've got her truly laid for them; may I just give her half a turn of the handles?'*
Chelmsford, who was near, gave permission for the range to be tested by a short burst, and the petty officer gave the handle two swift turns. The effect was devastating; a lane was cut clear through the Zulus.

Most of the warriors were now concealed by the long grass, and when they emerged, the distance had halved. The left horn of the *impi* was slightly in advance, and the north face of the laager was the first to feel the weight of the attack, as the extreme left began to work round the rear. The chest and right horn, coming down from Umisi hill were a little behind, but they rapidly reached the left and rear sides of the laager. As they came on, the warriors cried *I-ya-hlangena*, 'We have surrounded them.' The infantry companies within the square replied with a steady and deliberate volley firing, but even this, supplemented by the crackle of the Gatlings, failed to drown the shouts of the warriors.

The rocket tubes were situated at the front right angle of the laager. They were more likely to set the tents on fire and frighten the horses than do any serious execution upon the enemy, but
*Molyneux, W. C. F. *Campaigning in South Africa and Egypt*.

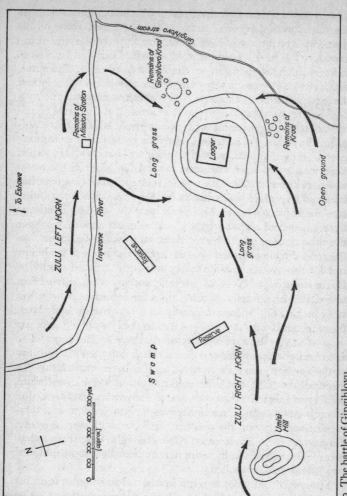

10 The battle of Gingihlovu

the Zulus were at first frightened by them. As the rockets skimmed over the grass, emitting tails of flame, some of the warriors were seen to fire at them, and those in the line of fire began to fall back. Seeing this, Chelmsford ordered Barrow to take out his horsemen and get the Zulus on the run. The move, however, was premature, for the warriors soon realised they had little to fear from the rockets, and turned on Barrow's men.

Since by now the laager was surrounded, the general feared that Barrow might be cut off and sent his ADC, Captain* William Molyneux, to recall him. Molyneux was only just in time, and the mounted men had to fight their way back with the loss of six horses killed or injured, and three riders wounded, Barrow amongst them. A Zulu shot at Molyneux at close quarters, but received a revolver bullet in the forehead; another put a bullet into the captain's horse, Lampas,† near the saddle. The beast faltered, picked up, and by a supreme effort carried his rider over the trench, where he collapsed, throwing Molyneux into the mud. Picking himself up, the captain despatched the horse, quickly removed the saddle and bridle, and staggered round the laager in search of Noot, his servant, and his other horse. Noot was sitting on a wagon, loading rifles for John Dunn, who was busy picking off Zulus with deadly accuracy. Seeing Molyneux, Noot 'beamed with joy' and pointed to the body of a forelooper who had been the first casualty on that side of the laager. The man had got in a panic when the attack commenced, and hid under a wagon, where he received a bullet in the head. Nearby, a Kaffir of the NNC lay under a commissariat wagon, snoring. A bullet had pierced a rum cask, and the native had rapidly drunk himself into a stupor. In another wagon, Norris-Newman, temporarily exchanging his pen for a rifle, and Palmer, a wagon conductor, were firing away. After the fight they went out to claim the spoils of war by stripping the clothing and weapons off two Zulus they had killed.

Molyneux told Noot to clean up the saddle and put it on his spare horse, and then climbed into the wagon with Dunn. 'I've picked out an *inDuna* or two,' was his only comment. The men in the wagons had the advantage of being able to shoot down at

---

* Later Major-General.
† Molyneux had named both his horses after equestrian diseases.

an angle, for the Zulus were by now on their stomachs, rising to their knees to fire. Many of the troops in the trench, unable to see the enemy in the long grass, had ceased firing, and were kneeling at the ready in case of a rush.

When his spare horse – Poll Evil – was saddled, Molyneux went to find Lord Chelmsford, passing on the way the 57th, now hotly engaged. Despite this, their volleys rang out with such disciplined regularity that they might have been at Aldershot. The native contingent presented a less soldierly spectacle. They were squatting between the trench and the wagons, and had been ordered to keep the muzzles of their rifles pointing sky-wards, and on no account to fire them. Their white officers were standing facing them, despite which rifle after rifle was dis-charged into the air at no great elevation. There then followed hard words and harder kicks.

Lord Chelmsford, quixotically wearing a red nightcap, was on foot, encouraging the men, and directing them to fire low. His staff were still on horseback, and it was a wonder that only Crealock had been hit, and slightly at that. Lieutenant-Colonel Northey was less lucky; shortly afterwards he was struck by a Martini bullet, causing a wound from which he died four days later.

Again and again the Zulus stormed towards the laager, only to be met with the same terrible volley fire they had already experienced at Isandhlwana. Some of the warriors came very close to the trench again, and one of the Gatlings was nearly taken – a Zulu actually fell dead against it. A little *uDibi* boy ran right through the fire and reached the trench. A bluejacket from HMS *Boadicea* grabbed him, beat him into submission and sat on him till the battle was over. The boy later became the ship's mascot, and entered the Royal Navy.

After an hour and a half, it was clear that the *impi* were wavering, so Chelmsford ordered Barrow out once more, plus the native contingent, to pursue. This time the Zulus did not turn to confront their antagonists, but fled as fast as they could, some towards Umisi hill, other across the Inyezane, many of them throwing away their weapons as they ran. The mounted infantry had been equipped with sabres, effective in the hands of regular cavalrymen, but more of an encumbrance to those not trained in swordplay. One of the colonial officers found himself in difficulties: a warrior turned at bay and snatched the sabre from his grip; but at that moment Sergeant Anderson, of the 5th Carbineers galloped up, ran the Zulu through, and rode on without pausing.

It had been impressed upon the infantry and sailors that they must not, under any circumstances, leave the laager; particularly severe punishment had been threatened to any blue-jacket who left his post. The sight of the retreating *impi*, hounded by the horsemen, was too much for the senior naval officer; forgetting his own orders, he called upon his flag-lieutenant and joined energetically in the pursuit, hacking and slashing in all directions. The sailors, mindful of the threatened penalties, never stirred, but yelled with delight, 'Go to it Admiral!' and, 'Now you've got 'em! Look out, sir, there's one to the right in the grass!' till they were all roaring with laughter.

At the same time, a more dramatic combat was being enacted. One Zulu refused to run away, but placed his back to a thorn bush and defied anyone to approach. A sergeant of the Scots Greys, who was an instructor to the mounted infantry, said, 'Leave him to me' and rode at the warrior. A circle of spectators formed to watch this single combat of mounted swordsman against spear and shield afoot. The sergeant was more skilful with his blade, but the Zulu was fitter and more agile. Every sabre cut was parried with the ox hide shield, till at last the swordsman used the point, and the gallant Zulu fell trans-fixed.

Zulu losses were heavy; 700 or more bodies were found scattered around the laager, and several hundred more were accounted for by the mounted men and Natal Kaffirs. Over 400 rifles, some of which bore the mark of the 24th Regiment, were picked up, and the sword which Lieutenant Porteous had worn at Isandhlwana was also recovered. British losses were two officers and eleven men dead, and four dozen wounded. Lord Chelmsford was triumphant: his concept of how to fight the war was vindicated and, having been in personal command, his honour was satisfied.

At Eshowe, twelve miles away, the crackle of small arms fire had just been audible. Pearson had been able to witness the distant battle through a telescope and then flash a congratulatory message by heliograph.

The next day Eshowe was relieved. Pearson, unable to contain his delight, marched out of the fort to meet the relieving column, and met Norris-Newman, who cried enthusiastically, 'First in Eshowe! Proud to be an Eshowian!' and galloped on to the fort. Pearson went on to meet Chelmsford, and together they rode back to the fort while the men of the garrison, after ten weeks of siege, cheered wildly, and the 91st Highlanders, colours flying, marched in to the skirl of *The Campbells are Coming*.

On 4 April, the garrison of Eshowe marched out towards the Tugela. The road was in an appalling state, and the men, not in the best of health, were slowed down by their wagons – 119 in all – and the presence of 120 sick, some of whom had to be carried in field ambulances. The relieving column followed a day later, and the Zulus fired the fort behind them. The march was a melancholy one. Two of the sick men died. On the night of the 6th, a picket of the 3rd/60th panicked on hearing a shot, and bolted back to the laager, closely followed by some of Dunn's scouts. The troops in the laager, mistaking the rush in the darkness for an attack, opened fire, killing one of the soldiers and wounding four others. They then went for the natives with fixed bayonets, killing three and wounding eight others before Dunn rushed up and stopped the slaughter. The sergeant of the picket was court-martialled and reduced to the ranks.

The track was littered with the debris of war: the decomposing bodies on the battlefield at Gingihlovu; abandoned wagons; and the graves of the men who had fallen at Inyezane on 22 January.

While the troops pushed slowly towards the Lower Drift, Chelmsford, with his staff, rode on ahead to Durban, which he reached on the 9th, in order to prepare for the second invasion of Zululand. From the colonial secretary of Cape Colony, the general received a congratulatory telegram:

Allow me to congratulate you upon your recent successful millitary operation . . . This ought to shut up some of the merciless critics at home . . . I hope the clouds are breaking now . . .

Chapter nine

Reorganisation

On his arrival in Durban on 9 April, Lord Chelmsford found the military situation in Natal materially altered. In addition to the reinforcements engaged in the relief of Eshowe, the rest of the troops sent out from England on receipt of the news of Isandhlwana had also arrived. Chelmsford now had at his disposal no fewer than fifteen British infantry battalions; two regular cavalry regiments, the 17th Lancers and the King's Dragoon Guards, who had brought their own horses from England; as well as the Naval Brigade, the various artillery units, mounted colonial volunteers and Natal Kaffirs. There were in all some 16,000 white troops, and 7,000 natives, plus a legion of civilian wagoners. On top of that, four major-generals had arrived in South Africa to command these forces.

There was no need for the second invasion of Zululand to be three-pronged as the first had been. Wood's experience at Kambula and his own at Gingihlovu had demonstrated to Chelmsford that to reach and destroy the Zulu capital a single strong column of all arms, as mobile as possible, was what was really needed. Too great a number of troops increased the problems of transport and supply out of all proportion to their usefulness. To this extent, the number of men now available to the general was an embarrassment rather than a help; gainful employment would have to be found for them and for the four major-generals, for whom, under the new plan of attack, there were too few duties.

Most senior of the four generals was the one sent by the Duke of Cambridge in response to Chelmsford's request for a senior officer to share the administrative responsibilities of command – Major-General the Honourable H. Clifford, VC, CB. Chelmsford appointed Clifford as Inspector General, putting him in control of the forces in Natal and on the lines of communication, with headquarters at Pietermaritzburg. The number of men under Clifford's command for this purpose was substantial. There were two companies of the 2nd/21st plus a general depot at Pietermaritzburg, and companies of the 58th at Durban and Ladysmith. At the Lower Tugela forts were the Naval Brigade and three or four companies of infantry from various regiments. The 2nd/24th had four companies at Dundee and another four split between Rorke's Drift and Helpmakaar. Eight companies of the 2nd/4th were distributed between Utrecht, Newcastle, Balte Spruit, Luneberg and Conference Hill, the latter supplemented by two squadrons of the King's Dragoon Guards. There was a half-company drawn from various units at Stanger, and two battalions of the Natal Native Contingent at Krantz Kop.

Despite the number of generals now available, Chelmsford had no wish to relieve of his command such an excellent officer and experienced Zulu-fighter as Evelyn Wood; so on 10 April Wood was given the local rank of brigadier-general and confirmed in his command. His column was now known as the Flying Column, and to supplement the 1st/13th and 90th Regiments, already with him, Chelmsford sent four companies of the 80th, plus the 10/7 RA, four Gatling guns and additional mounted men.

The remainder of the Field Force was organised in a way which clearly demonstrated the strength of Chelmsford's new army. The 1st Division was given to Major-General H. H. Crealock, CB, and was divided into two brigades. The 1st Brigade, under Colonel Pearson, was composed of eight companies of the 2nd/3rd, six of the 88th, and eight of the 99th Regiments. The 2nd Brigade, commanded by Lieutenant-Colonel Clark, comprised eight companies of the 57th, seven of the 3rd/60th Rifles, and eight of the 91st Highlanders. The two brigades were accompanied by divisional troops including a naval brigade, two NNC battalions, mounted volunteers, engineers and thirteen guns.

To Major-General E. Newdigate went the 2nd Division, also with two brigades, plus a cavalry brigade, under Major-General Marshall, consisting of the 1st Dragoon Guards, the 17th Lancers and a number of native horsemen. Colonel Glyn commanded the 1st Brigade, composed of six companies of the 2nd/21st and six of the 58th, while Colonel Collingwood led the 2nd Brigade, made up of seven 1st/24th and six 94th Regiment companies.

The size and organisation of the army was impressive; in fact, several weeks elapsed before all the troops could be assembled in their respective divisions and brigades. A further delay of six weeks was occasioned by the troop movements necessitated by Chelmsford's plan for the second invasion.

The general had decided to advance upon the Zulu capital at Ulundi with a single column, composed of the 2nd Division and the Flying Column, using the 1st Division to stage a diversionary feint, to keep Cetewayo guessing and his *impis* split. As far as the choice of routes into Zululand was concerned, Chelmsford had three choices. He could cross the Tugela at the Lower Drift, as Pearson's column had done, and approach Ulundi from the south; he could cross the Tugela in the north, at Landman's Drift, and follow the route that Wood's original force would have followed; or he could cross at Rorke's Drift. Chelmsford chose the northern route, no doubt being swayed by the consideration that he could thus get the 2nd Division across the White Umfolozi and its tributary streams much higher up, where they were smaller, and then move more or less parallel with the main streams. The Rorke's Drift course does not seem to have been considered; perhaps its associations with the original Central Column were too painful to contemplate. Nevertheless, his decision involved not only considerable delay in mounting the second offensive, but enormous problems in transporting sufficient supplies to the north.

Chelmsford's orders to Crealock were precise as far as they went: the 1st Division was to advance from Fort Pearson on the Lower Drift, destroy the military kraal at Emangwene, said to hold 1,000 huts, and clear the surrounding district. When this was done, the kraal at Undi, ten miles from Emangwene, was also to be razed. Chelmsford thought it probable that Cetewayo would contest these proceedings, taking some of the pressure off the 2nd Division. To enable him to operate against Emangwene and Undi, some forty miles into Zululand, Crealock was instructed to establish a strong entrenched post between the

Tugela and the Umfolozi, with a halfway depot on the Amiti-kulu River. Ultimately, Chelmsford hoped that Crealock would be able to advance farther and set up a fortified post and supply depot in the vicinity of St. Pauls, a mission station fifteen miles north of Eshowe. However, he wrote in his orders to Crealock that, having destroyed Emangwene and Undi, '. . . the Major-General will have to decide for himself as to what further operations are possible or desirable'.

Crealock started for the Lower Drift on 16 April, to organise the advance of his division. It was a formidable task: he had large numbers of men and inadequate transport, most of which had been allocated to the 2nd Division. His supplies amounted to some 1,200 wagonloads, for which he had only 250 wagons. The grazing for the oxen was sparse, and very soon all used up along the track. The 2nd Brigade moved quickly to the Inyezane, but the 1st became bogged down on the Tugela.

Without too much difficulty, Crealock established his inter-mediate base on the Amitikulu – and named it Fort Crealock. On 21 April, the first supply convoy set out, 110 wagons in all, but in mid-June, by which time an adequate supply of provisions had been established at the depot, overwork and poor grazing had so weakened the oxen that even light loads had to be drawn by double teams, which even so could manage ever shorter and shorter marches. It was 19 June before Crealock's entire division was established on the Inyezane, at what was tactfully named Fort Chelmsford. By this time, 497 officers and men of the 1st Division had been invalided back to Natal with enteric fever and seventy-one had died. Fortunately, no Zulus had been en-countered. Crealock goaded his column – 'Crealock's Crawlers' – a few more miles to a site on the coast, where supplies could be landed from the sea, so avoiding the necessity of relying on a long overland supply route, which was in danger of breaking down completely. Here the 1st Division camped, and played little part in the coming campaign.

Newdigate's 2nd Division, meanwhile, with Marshall's cavalry brigade, had been slowly moving northwards by way of Greytown, Escourt and Ladysmith. Lord Chelmsford's diffi-culties now seemed to multiply. The condition of men and horses gave some cause for anxiety. The reinforcements sent out from England were as yet inexperienced. Their officers had arrived with vast amounts of impedimenta, totally unsuited to conditions in the field, which had to be discarded. The ranks of some regiments were filled out with men freshly recruited or collected from depots in order to bring their units up to strength, and many were very young. 'The boys that now fill our battalions add very much to my anxiety,' wrote Chelmsford to the Duke of Cambridge. They required a great deal of training and toughening.

The same thing applied to the horses of the two regular cavalry regiments. The animals had come through the long voyage quite well, and looked in good condition when Chelmsford inspected them, but appearances were deceptive. To start with, they were unaccustomed to graze for themselves, having hitherto been fed on cut fodder. Then they were expected to carry a saddle and equipment weighing 100lb – in addition to a trooper – a weight which astounded the colonial horsemen. When the dragoons and lancers left Durban on 17 April, they could at first only cover ten miles a day, while the horses slowly got into condition.

A new and quite unexpected problem sprang up in the form of Major-General Clifford, who had been sent out to relieve Chelmsford of some of his burdens. The origin of Clifford's difficult and even insubordinate behaviour seems to have stemmed from his resentment of the fact that his sphere of responsibility as Inspector General of Base and Lines of Communications was limited to Natal, and stopped at the Zulu border. It should, he felt, extend along the entire line of communications, through Zululand and up to the advancing columns. From his base at Pietermaritzburg, this would, of course, have been quite impracticable, even if desirable.

Clifford first of all picked upon Crealock, an officer of equal rank, and did so in a quite extraordinary fashion. He sent not an officer, but Norris-Newman, the *Standard* correspondent, to visit the camp of the 1st Division on the Inyezane, and to 'inquire into its state'. Not surprisingly, the camp was, as Crealock himself would have admitted, in a mess. Norris-Newman wrote a report to this effect and sent it to Clifford, who returned it to Crealock with a note attached saying: 'My dear Crealock. Will you kindly have these statements of the correspondent of the *Standard* inquired into . . .' Crealock, furious wrote, 'Read and returned' on the back, and sent it back to Clifford. To his brother he wrote that he proposed to ignore Clifford and his communications.

The matter did not rest there, however, for on 1 May Clifford sent ten inspecting officers from the commissariat and ordnance departments to examine the workings of the 1st Division's transport. Crealock, as he again told his brother, 'cut up rusty', telling the inspectors that he had no need of wet-nurses; but this grievance continued to simmer.

The man to suffer most from Clifford's attentions was Colonel Strickland, the Commissary-General, who was doing his best in very difficult conditions, with an overworked and understaffed department, to organise as much transport as he could as efficiently as possible. Clifford's behaviour might have gone unchecked had he confined his attentions to his subordinates and peers, but soon he was criticising Lord Chelmsford, too.

On 28 April, for example, Clifford sent Chelmsford a peremptory telegram: 'Harrison and Heimages reports on roads should be sent on to me. Their reports must not be acted on without my order or that of my officer or confusion will result'. He wrote freely to the general, offering gratuitous advice on sundry topics, punctuating them with unctuous phrases such as: 'Do not think, my dear Lord Chelmsford, that I have taken a one-sided view of this or any other question in this war . . .' or '. . . my one sole object in view is to do what I think right as a Christian and a soldier'. Lord Chelmsford displayed great forbearance towards Clifford, and the incident which at last brought that officer a stern rebuke did not come until the closing stage of the war.

But all these problems and annoyances paled to insignificance besides the greatest and most serious difficulty, that of transport and supply. This, the Field Force's recurring nightmare, slowed the concentration of the 2nd Division to a crawl, and opened Chelmsford to charges of dilatoriness at home.

The transport problem had several aspects. The war had placed a severe strain upon the resources of Natal, so that the supply of wagon conductors, native forelopers, wagons and draught oxen was virtually exhausted. In addition, the roads had deteriorated, the drifts were dissolving into mud, and pasturage near the tracks was almost non-existent. This state of affairs was naturally costly. An indemnity of £20 was payable on any ox that died and they were now dropping by the score. Replacements were obtained only at greatly inflated prices.

Chelmsford appealed to the civil authorities for help, but they were unco-operative, to the point of deliberate obstruction. Both Wood and Crealock had complained bitterly of this. To enable him to obtain by compulsion the transport that the colonists would not provide voluntarily, Chelmsford begged Bulwer to place Natal under martial law. Bulwer refused. Marshall, the cavalry general, also had an interview with the lieutenant-governor, which grew rather heated. Bulwer promised to help to round up some native drivers, but actually confined himself to appealing to the colonists to sell draught animals to the army. The result was nearly 700 extra oxen, but this was by no means the end of the story, as Chelmsford wrote to the Duke of Cambridge on 14 May:

Oxen bought in one part die if worked in another. They thrive on grass in one district and fall sick if kept long on different grass. They require to be carefully worked and driven, or they are certain to die or become inefficient, and if exposed in winter to the cold S.E. wind, even in the day time great loss of life is certain to ensue.

In the same letter, Chelmsford candidly stated that '. . . our transport has broken down completely for want of officers who have been properly educated in that branch of the service'. Colonel Strickland, though working manfully, was badly served by his subordinates, who displayed no energy, no resourcefulness, were afraid of responsibility, and who thought only of issuing instructions and never of seeing that they were carried out.

Lord Chelmsford had to contend with another burden as unwelcome as it was unusual. Amongst the reinforcements sent out from England was Louis Napoleon, the Prince Imperial of France. The presence of this young man with the army had come about by curious circumstances. Exiled from France after the Franco-Prussian War, the French royal family had settled in England, where Louis had received part of his education at the Royal Military Academy at Woolwich, from which he had passed out with conspicuous success. He had not been allowed to take up a commission in the army, and was obliged to live in a state of bored exile. With the news of Isandhlwana, Louis had sought permission to go out to South Africa. The commander-in-chief was agreeable, but Disraeli, who could foresee the possible repercussions if the heir to the French throne were to serve as a British officer, forbade it. 'Nothing', he said, 'could be more injudicious than the whole affair'. The prime minister, however, reckoned without the personal intervention of the Queen and the prince's mother, and was forced in the end to give way: Louis should go after all.

The prime minister, finding the matter arranged over his head, wrote in disgust to Salisbury on 28 February:

I an quite mystified about that little abortion, the Prince Imperial. I thought we had agreed not to sanction his adventure? Instead of that he has royal audiences previous to departure, is reported to be a future staff officer . . .

And to a friend, Disraeli wrote:

Well, my conscience is clear. I did all I could to stop his going. But what can you do when you have two obstinate women to deal with? I only hope the French will be as overjoyed as everybody else.

They were not. The question was, in what capacity should Louis go? It hardly seemed desirable that a Napoleon should serve as a junior officer in a battery, and even less that he should be put in a position where he might be killed. The commander-in-chief conceived an ingenious idea: the prince need not go out to Zululand as a serving officer, but as a *spectator*. He could thus see something of the coming campaign, live the life of a soldier and satisfy his thirst for adventure without incurring the slightest risk. Accordingly, on 25 February, the duke wrote to Chelmsford:

This letter will be forwarded to you by the Prince Imperial, who is going out on his own account to see as much as he can of the coming campaign in Zululand. He is extremely anxious to go out and wanted employment in our army, but the Government did not consider that this could be sanctioned, but have sanctioned me only to you and Sir Bartle Frere to say that if you shew him kindness and tender him a position to see as much as he can with the columns in the Field I hope you will do so . . . My only anxiety on his conduct would be that he is too *plucky* and *go ahead*.

To Frere, his royal highness stressed the fact that Louis was going out strictly 'in the capacity of a spectator'.

Louis presented himself before Lord Chelmsford on the general's return from the relief of Eshowe, giving him the letter from the Duke of Cambridge, and another from Sir Lintorn Simmons, the Governor of the Royal Military Academy, who commended his sometime pupil in the following terms:

He is very intelligent, thoroughly amenable to discipline, very zealous and active, a quick and accurate observer, and a good rider; he can sketch ground tolerably and gives every promise of being a good officer. Having been attached to batteries during two series of manoeuvres, he has a fair knowledge of the movement of troops. His only fault is that which is common to youth, viz: that he is rather impulsive, but of this I have little doubt he will soon get better.

It is not surprising that Chelmsford was nonplussed by the arrival of the prince and his letters of introduction. The one from the duke seemed contradictory: on the one hand it stated that Louis should be given a 'position'; and, on the other, emphasised that the prince was a private individual, a sightseer only, and not a British officer. Simmons's letter suggested that Louis would make a good officer if given the chance. The only things quite clear to Chelmsford were that the prince was thirsting for active employment, and that he was likely to get himself into a scrape if at all possible.

The general offered Louis the command of a squadron of irregulars, but the prince had the sense to turn this down, as he told his mother in a letter. At a loss, Chelmsford suggested that Louis should join his personal staff, and this the prince agreed to do. Louis's presence was certainly an embarrassment, but there was, when Chelmsford reflected upon it, a brighter side, as he wrote to Sir Lintorn Simmons:

The Prince Imperial has consented to accompany me into the field, and without putting him in orders, I have arranged that he shall be considered as one of my personal staff. I hear that he is quite delighted at being so employed; and at all events his desire to serve under my command is a set-off to those who consider I am quite unfit for my present command . . .

On 2 May, Chelmsford left Dundee, the base of Newdigate's 2nd Division, and rode with his staff to visit Wood and the Flying Column at Kambula. Here Louis, enjoying every moment of the rough soldier's life he was leading – he was, as somebody said, 'no feather bed soldier' – met his old artillery friends, Bigge and Slade, who had been present at the battle of Kambula, and was thrilled by their accounts of the fight. Chelmsford then moved back to Utrecht, where he established a temporary headquarters, remaining there until the 24th.

The general had decided that Newdigate's column should cross the border into Zululand at Koppie Allein, twelve miles to the east of Landman's Drift on the Buffalo. A depot was accordingly formed at Koppie Allein, and stores were assembled there from Landman's Drift and Conference Hill. By the end of May, the 2nd Division was gathered on the Blood ready for the invasion, while Wood's Flying Column, which had vacated Kambula on 5 May, had moved to Munhla Hill, some twenty-two miles south of Kambula and thirteen miles east of Conference Hill, from where it could co-operate with Newdigate.

At Utrecht, Chelmsford appointed as his action quartermaster general Colonel Richard Harrison, an engineer with experience in China and in the Indian Mutiny. Harrison's functions in his new capacity were to see that the appropriate supplies and transport for the 2nd Division were forthcoming when required; and, secondly, to select and scout the route by which the division would enter Zululand, and to choose suitable camping sites for each night's halt.

For this vital job Harrison had no help save that of a single corporal, so Chelmsford attached to him Lieutenant J. B. Carey, 98th Regiment, one of the large number of supernumerary special service officers having no particular duties. Even with Carey's assistance, however, Harrison would still be under-staffed for the job in hand, so the general decided to give him the Prince Imperial as well. Chelmsford would thereby be relieved of the task of looking after Louis himself, and at the same time, the prince would be gainfully employed in a position with no risks attached. That, at least, was what Lord Chelmsford fondly imagined.

One of Harrison's duties was to reconnoitre the route of the 2nd Division into Zululand. Wood, to the south-east, was em-ploying Colonel Buller and his mounted men to do the same for the Flying Column, and Harrison decided that he would accom-pany Buller on his next reconnaissance. On 13 May, Harrison rode to join Buller, Chelmsford having given his permission for Louis to go too. With an escort of 200 men of the Frontier Light Horse and Edendale contingent, led by the redoubtable Buller, the prince could hardly come to any harm.

The following day the patrol crossed the Blood River at Koppie Allein, and Louis was at last in Zululand. To be in enemy country! It was magnificent. Wearing the sword that Bonaparte had carried at Austerlitz, the prince was almost be-side himself. Once or twice Zulus were seen in the distance, and Louis was off in pursuit. 'Chops' Mossop, of the Frontier Light Horse, remembered these incidents clearly:

When we were on the move during the day, riding in half-sections, he [the prince] was a real terror; if any Zulus were seen – and they were usually on the slope of a hill – he would dart out of the rank, his servant behind him, and race sword in hand to get at them. His great ambition was to come to close quarters, and try his sword against shield and spear. He did not appear to care whether he was obeying orders from Buller or not.

Twice Buller had to order troopers of the Frontier Light Horse to chase after Louis and bring him back. When caught, he would smile and say, 'Thank you, thank you!' and then, re-placing his sword, calmly ride back. He did not seem to mind the wigging he received from Buller as a result. The prince clearly intended to be a very active 'spectator'.

Louis was elated by these encounters, and also by the fact

that the hill near where he had chased the Zulus was named Napoleon Koppie by the men. For his part, Buller was disgusted. He was conducting a reconnaissance, not a Zulu-hunt.

The scouting party had found a route suitable for Wood's column, and by the 16th had returned to its starting point, with Buller vowing that he would never again permit Louis to accompany him. Wood hailed the prince jovially: 'Well, sir, you've not been assegaied yet?'

'Not yet', replied the prince characteristically, 'but while I've no desire to be killed, if I had to fall I should prefer an assegai to a bullet. It would prove that we'd been at close quarters.'*

The problem of the route for Newdigate's division had still to be settled, and Colonel Harrison decided upon a second, smaller scouting expedition. He sent Louis back to Conference Hill, declining to take him unless Chelmsford himself sanctioned the move. In order to obtain permission, the prince rode all the way to Utrecht and back in time to join Harrison before he started out.

The escort on this occasion was drawn from the Natal Horse led by Commandant Bettington, who to Louis's amazement disdained swords and carried a riding crop instead. Lieutenant Carey accompanied the patrol, and he and the prince spent some time sketching the ground.

On the second day out, the party was fired upon by a few Zulus, concealed in the rocks by a kraal on a hillside. Bettington ordered his troopers in to the attack, and Louis, excited at being under fire for the first time, charged ahead, sword in hand, seeking a warrior to engage in hand-to-hand combat. There was more shooting as the Zulus retired, but nobody was hit. The patrol fired the kraal, after finding in it some of the stores looted from Isandhlwana.

Harrison wished to push on a little farther to the east, in order to verify some points on his maps; then, late in the afternoon, the patrol turned for home. After another brief encounter with a small party of Zulus and a long ride through the night, they were back at Conference Hill by breakfast time, having found a practicable route for the 2nd Division. Harrison, however, could have saved himself the trouble, for Buller found another

* John, K. *The Prince Imperial.*

suitable route slightly to the north, and it was this that Lord Chelmsford elected to use.

By the time Harrison, Carey and Louis had ridden back to Utrecht, Buller had lodged a complaint with the general regarding the prince's conduct on the patrol; as a result of which orders were given to Harrison, who passed them to Louis in writing, that he was not in future to leave the camp without a strong escort.

The prince did in fact succeed in riding out on another foray into hostile territory, accompanied by a number of irregulars and by Captain W. C. Molyneux, of the 22nd Regiment. Since Molyneux was one of Chelmsford's ADCs, the general presumably knew that the prince was out. As they were riding slowly homeward, Molyneux reverted to the subject of Louis's conduct out on the patrol with Harrison and Bettington. Why, Molyneux inquired, had the prince rashly dashed out in front and risked his life in order to get to grips with a few Zulus whose deaths, after all, would have made not the slightest difference to the outcome of the campaign.

'You are right, I suppose,' replied the prince, 'but I could not help it. I feel I must do something.' As Louis spoke, a shot rang out to their left. Nothing was to be seen; the trooper who had fired was reloading, riding quietly on without hurrying or dismounting. From this, Molyneux concluded that the man had hit whatever it was he had fired at. Not so the prince, who instantly drew his sword and went at full gallop in the direction of the trooper. Molyneux, without a hope of catching him, and afraid that in the gathering twilight Louis's horse should stumble, cried, 'Prince, I must order you to come back.' Louis 'pulled up at once, saluted, returned his sword and said nothing for a minute; then broke out, "It seems I am never to be without a nurse"; and a moment after, "Oh, forgive me; but don't you think you are a little phlegmatic?"'

After one or other of these adventures, the prince remarked to Archibald Forbes, the newspaper man: 'Such skirmishes suit my taste exactly, yet I should be *au désespoir* did I think I should be killed in one.'

While Louis was enjoying his forays into Zululand, the final preparations for the invasion were being made and, by the end of May, Lord Chelmsford was ready to embark upon the final stage of the war. But, at the very moment of his doing so, a fresh disaster struck, as fearful in its way as Isandhlwana.

The Prince Imperial was dead.

Chapter ten
The Prince Imperial

Sunday, 1 June, was the date selected for the commencement of the advance. The 2nd Division was to move some seven miles into enemy territory and bivouac on the first night near Itelezi Hill. The Flying Column, advancing on a nearly convergent course, would camp only a mile away. Cavalry patrols were to scout the ground ten miles beyond these camp sites in the direction of the second night's bivouac.

Harrison, mindful of the need to keep the Prince Imperial out of trouble when in enemy territory, had decided to employ him in sketching the route to be taken by the division; but at some time during the evening of 31 May, the prince went to Harrison's tent and sought permission to advance beyond the area to be traversed next day. Harrison wrote later:

I saw no objection to this providing he took with him the usual escort. Many of us had been over the ground, and we knew that there was no 'impi' in the neighbourhood. Moreover, I thought that the cavalry which accompanied the division would be extended over the country far in advance of the camp, so I gave permission.*

Harrison specified that the escort was to consist of half a dozen troopers of Bettington's Horse, plus six mounted natives of the Edendale contingent.

Shortly after the prince left Harrison's tent, Lieutenant Carey appeared, and asked if he might accompany Louis on the morrow in order to complete and verify some sketches he had made on his previous scouting of the country beyond Itelezi Hill. Harrison, in his memoirs, states that he replied in the affirmative, and that he added that Carey 'could look after the prince and see he did not get into any trouble'. The colonel then gave

* Harrison, R. *Recollections of a Life in the British Army.*

Carey a note authorising him to request the escort of six white troopers and six Basutos from the cavalry brigade-major. At neither meeting did Harrison specify who was to command the party. The prince, in fact, held no official position in the army, although he wore the uniform of an officer in the Royal Artillery.

Archibald Forbes was with Herbert Stewart, the cavalry brigade-major, when Carey appeared. The note did not state that the escort was for the Prince Imperial, and Carey did not mention the fact. Nor did he demur at the size of the escort – if he had, Stewart might have provided a stronger party.

At 9am on 1 June, the six men of Bettington's Horse reported for escort duty. Senior amongst them was Corporal Grubb, who after farming for years in Natal, spoke fluent Zulu. With him were five troopers – Rogers, Cochrane, Willis, Abel and Le Tocq. The latter, a Channel Islander, spoke French. They were accompanied by a friendly Zulu acting as guide. The six Basutos failed to appear. The 2nd Division's camp was in a state of some confusion, as tents were struck and wagons loaded, and it seems that the troopers reported to the wrong tent. Stewart told Carey that he would send them on, as soon as they appeared, and that in the meantime they could call upon other mounted Basutos scouting along the line of advance.

As Louis, Carey and their seven men, accompanied by the prince's dog, set out across good open grass country, they were at first by no means alone, for Newdigate's column was already in motion and the landscape was dotted with troops moving towards Itelezi.

Two of Louis's horses had died, and that morning, with little choice left to him, he was riding a big awkward grey, a powerful beast, but an inveterate 'buck-jumper', and said to be timid under fire. The prince was warned against him, but he was a superb horseman and would not admit to being unable to manage the animal. Neither Louis nor Carey carried a Martini-Henry carbine, as did the troopers; they were armed only with swords and revolvers, which were attached to their saddles and not, as they should have been, on their persons. Had the prince been mounted on a different horse, or had he been wearing his revolver, the outcome of the day might have been different.*

* Ashe and Wyatt-Edgell. *The Story of the Zulu Campaign.*

After a while, Louis's party came up with Harrison and Major F. W. Grenfell, 3rd/60th Rifles, the staff officer of the day, who were on their way to the next camp-site at Itelezi. The colonel noted the absence of the Basutos, but Carey told him that they were to pick up half a dozen from the mounted patrols ahead, and with this Harrison was satisfied. The two parties rode on together as far as Itelezi, where Harrison began his camping and watering arrangements for the column. Grenfell, however, decided to go on a little way with the others. He rode out in front, talking with Louis, while Carey came behind with the men. After several miles Grenfell turned back and, as he bade farewell, said to Louis: 'Take care of yourself, Prince, and don't get shot.' To this Louis replied, pointing to Carey: 'Oh no! He'll take very good care that nothing happens to me.'

Then, in the equivocal words of the *Official Narrative*, the Prince Imperial 'moved on with his eight companions to carry out the reconnaissance on which he was engaged'.

If the idea had ever entered Lieutenant Carey's head that it was he who commanded the party, now was the moment for him to exercise his authority. The six Basutos sent galloping after them by the cavalry brigade-major had not appeared – they had stopped at Itelezi Hill. The mounted scouting parties which had been in evidence farther back had disappeared. Carey should have insisted on finding one of them and getting the six extra men, but he – or the prince – decided against it.

For seven or eight miles the party rode along the ridge towards the valley of the Ityotyosi River. When, at about half an hour after noon, a flat-topped hill was reached at the end of the ridge, it was Louis who gave the order to off-saddle. Then, seeing a deserted kraal a couple of miles ahead and below them, in the valley of the Ityotyosi, he changed his mind and told the men merely to slacken their girths for a few moments. He said to Carey, 'It is hardly worth while to off-saddle for a quarter of an hour. We shall go down to the hut by the river, where the men can get wood and water and cook something.'

Carey quite rightly objected to this suggestion, which would place the party in a position from which they would be unable to keep the surrounding countryside under observation. But Louis made his wish known in a very 'authoritative' manner, and Carey allowed himself to be overruled.

After fifteen minutes, the men retightened their saddle girths and the party rode down towards the kraal, which they reached about three o'clock, without having seen any signs of the enemy. The kraal consisted of a circular cattle enclosure with a stone wall roughly four feet high, around which were grouped five empty beehive huts. From the kraal, two footpaths ran north for 200 yards to a donga, which they crossed. Between the kraal and the donga the ground was devoid of cover, but to the south, east and west, long tambookie grass grew right up to the huts, and beyond this, to the east and west, were patches of mealies.

It was evident that the kraal had been recently occupied, for there was a dog prowling about, and on the ground outside one of the huts were the fresh remains of food. The ashes in one of the fireplaces were still warm. Carey and Louis, however, having seen no signs of any inhabitants as they descended the hill, assumed with fatal carelessness that there were, in fact, no Zulus in the vicinity. With a staggering disregard for common-sense military precautions, they posted no sentries and made no attempt to examine the donga, the tambookie grass or the mealie patches.

The horses were by this time unsaddled and knee-haltered, again on Louis's orders. Then, while the Zulu scout went down to the river for water and two of the troopers got a fire going, the prince lay down at the door of one of the huts, complaining of feeling unwell. Coffee, perhaps, revived him, for he and Carey were soon busily engaged upon their maps and sketches, while discussing the military exploits of Louis's great forbear. The men lay at their ease, smoking and eating.

Just after 3.30, Carey put it to the prince that they should saddle-up and move on, but again allowed himself to be overruled: Louis declared that they should wait ten minutes more. At this moment the guide reported that he had seen a Zulu moving over the hill. Louis was unable to understand what was said, so Corporal Grubb was called upon to interpret. Accounts differ as to what happened next: some say that the prince immediately gave the order to saddle-up, but that there was a delay because the horses had strayed despite being knee-haltered;

another version appears in *The Story of the Zulu Campaign*, published the year after the war, and written by two officers serving with the Field Force – Ashe and Wyatt-Edgell.* According to this, Louis looked at his watch, and seeing that it was ten minutes to four, said to the men: 'You can give your horses ten minutes more.'

Whatever the truth of the matter, there was a delay of at least ten minutes from the time the hostile Zulu was sighted to the troopers catching their horses and saddling-up.

Carey was first in the saddle, while Louis went through the formal routine of mounting the men. 'Prepare to mount,' he ordered, and the troopers placed their left feet in the near stirrups. Then, at the precise moment the prince said, 'Mount!' a tremendous volley crashed out from the tambookie grass and some thirty or forty Zulus charged out of cover, shouting the war-cry '*uSuthu!*'

All the men save Rogers, whose horse had strayed farther than the rest, were now more or less in their saddles. Grubb was not very firmly up and, as his horse galloped off, he saw Rogers fire with his carbine – the only shot fired by the escort during the entire episode. The luckless Rogers was then swiftly speared.

Le Tocq had mounted, but in the struggle to do so had dropped his carbine, and he dismounted to retrieve it. Flinging himself on his horse, which bolted like the rest, he lay across the saddle trying to regain his seat. Carey was going at full gallop in the direction of the donga.

The prince, like Rogers, had failed to mount. His horse panicked at the sound of the shooting and dashed off, with Louis clinging to the saddle holster, half carried and half dragged along, desperately trying to secure a hold that would enable him to spring up into the saddle. Le Tocq, still sprawled across his horse's back, tore past the prince, crying out, as he recalled, either, '*Dépêchez-vous, monsieur, de monter!*' or, '*Dépêchez-vous, Vôtre Altesse, s'il vous plaît!*'† By a curious chance, these, the last words Louis heard from his comrades, were in his native tongue.

* Major Ashe actually published the book; Wyatt-Edgell was killed with the 17th Lancers at Ulundi.
† Whitton, F. E. *Service Trials and Tragedies.*

The Zulus were still firing after them, as they headed for the donga and yelling '*Usuta!*' ('Cowards!'). Trooper Abel, just in front of Grubb, was struck in the back and fell from his horse. Then Le Tocq passed the corporal, shouting, 'Stick firm to your horse, boy, and put the spurs in. The prince is down.' Grubb then looked behind him and saw Louis, still clinging to the holster, trampled on by his horse. Grubb's mount then leapt into the donga and the corporal, dropping his Martini-Henry in the effort to remain in the saddle, saw no more. Trooper Willis had seen both Abel and the prince go down.

Louis's horse had dragged him 200 yards before the strap of the holster parted. (It was later examined, and the material and workmanship were found to be defective.) Once more on his feet, the prince was now alone, armed only with his sword. He started to run, but the Zulus were rapidly upon him and he was surrounded. There was a brief fight, and then the Prince Imperial died in a welter of assegai thrusts.

The survivors scrambled across the donga at widely separated points. When he had galloped off, Carey had shouted out a single order: 'Bear to the left,' and the troopers now rallied round him. Of the Zulu guide there was no sign. The prince's horse was seen coming out of the watercourse, and Grubb caught and mounted him.

The entire episode had probably taken less than two minutes, and so far it had been a question of *sauve qui peut*. 'Where is the English iron nerve that is proof against the panic of a moment?' thundered Ashe and Wyatt-Edgell, after the event. 'Where are the guardians of England's princely guest? All have lost their courage and their manhood.' Such reactions were hardly just. What, in that brief moment, could Carey or anyone else have done, struggling as they were with their own frightened horses?

The unfortunate Carey, having committed the cardinal error of allowing the party to enter the kraal, was now on the horns of a dilemma, quite aside from the fact that the Zulus were now rapidly working round his depleted patrol. It seemed evident that the prince, Abel and Rogers must be dead; as the Zulus seldom left any wounded. What was Carey's duty at that moment? To go back and establish beyond doubt what had happened? Or did his first obligation lie with the survivors?

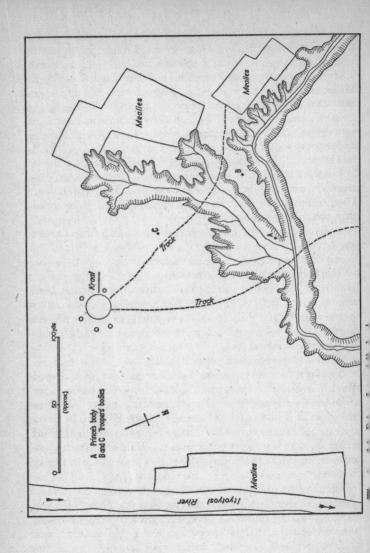

Meolies

Meolies

Track

.C

Krool

Track

.B

A.

100 yds

50 (approx)

N

A Prince's body
B and C Troopers' bodies

Meolies

Itvolyosi River

Carey decided that to go back would be unjustifiably risky. The five survivors therefore turned their horses to the west and rode as fast as they could towards Itelezi Hill.

About halfway between the kraal and the camp, Wood and Buller, riding with a small escort, encountered Carey. It is from their accounts that the details of this painful meeting derive.

'Why', Buller said to Wood, 'the man rides as if the Kaffirs were after him.' He then asked Carey, who by this time was some way ahead of his men, what was wrong.

'The prince, the Prince Imperial is killed!' blurted out Carey.

'Where are your men, sir? How many did you lose?' demanded Buller, to which the lieutenant replied, 'I don't know.' Then Buller, who could feel only contempt for this craven display, returned:

'You deserve to be shot, and I hope you will be. I could shoot you myself.'

The three officers and their men then rode on towards Itelezi, which they reached at about 7pm.

Carey informed Harrison of the dreadful news. Harrison then went to Lord Chelmsford's tent; the general was so shaken by this disaster that he slumped white and shaking into a chair, his face covered by his hands. Harrison left Chelmsford, who forbade an immediate rescue party, and went to see General Marshall, commander of the cavalry brigade.

Harrison put his head inside the tent and said in a strained voice, 'Good God! The Prince Imperial is killed!' Nobody, for a moment, took him seriously; Harrison was known to have an odd sense of humour. Lord Downe, Marshall's ADC, threw a piece of bread at him, and Stewart, the brigade-major, laughed aloud. But Forbes, the newspaper man, could see from the expression on Harrison's face in the sunset light in the doorway that he was not in jest.

The force that assembled at 5am next morning to go out and retrieve Louis's remains presented a curious contrast to his tiny escort of the previous day. The 17th Lancers were paraded, together with the colonial horsemen. There was an ambulance unit, and a battalion of the NNC, which caused so much confusion that the force did not march out of camp till nearly seven o'clock.

The body of Trooper Abel was found first, lying midway between the donga and the kraal, naked and horribly mutilated. Rogers' remains were nearby, with the stomach slashed open.

It was Captain Cochrane of the Edendale contingent who found the prince. He was lying on his back, naked save for a golden chain with some medallions around his neck. From the state of the ground, it was clear that he had fought desperately. His body bore seventeen assegai wounds, five of which were severe enough to have been fatal, including one in his right eye that had probably reached the brain, and another to his heart. One thrust had penetrated right through the body and come out of the back. Nearby lay the butchered body of his terrier, and a single blue sock, with the letter N embroidered upon it.

The body of the prince was wrapped in a sheet and carried back to the camp on a stretcher made from a blanket and four lances. As arrangements were made for the body to be taken to Pietermaritzburg and on to Durban, prior to its shipment to Cape Town and England, Chelmsford must have known and dreaded the reaction that was bound to follow. Louis had been the guest of England. He had come to South Africa with the Queen's blessing, as a spectator. In his moment of need a British officer had abandoned him. For Chelmsford, it would be like having to live down a second Isandhlwana. In fact, the death of the Prince Imperial caught the public imagination in a way that the previous disaster had not, and the outcry was worse. In a letter to Frere, Chelmsford gave vent to his only, belated, protest about being required to assume the burden of responsibility for the prince in the first place: 'I have always felt that it was somewhat unfair to saddle me with the responsibility which naturally would be attached to such a charge,' he wrote, and added, with a note of pathetic resignation, 'but I had to accept it with all the rest.'

Within the Field Force, the feeling against Harrison was strong. Against Carey it was intense; he had, the officer corps felt, brought them all into disrepute by his cowardly action. For a week Carey managed to resist the pressure and continue his normal duties; then he requested that the facts of the matter be examined by a court of inquiry. He was suspended from duty, and on 12 June, was court-martialled.

His defence consisted of trying to shift the entire blame for the tragedy upon the prince. Harrison, Carey alleged, had not charged him with command of the patrol, and had even suggested that he should not interfere with the prince. It had been Louis's patrol which he, Carey, had merely accompanied for purposes of sketching. It was Louis who had refused to wait for the six Basutos; Louis who had decided upon the kraal as a halting place; Louis who had failed to post lookouts.

But it was of no use. Carey was found guilty of misbehaviour in the face of the enemy, and ordered back to England immediately. Ironically, while these proceedings were in progress, he was gazetted captain.

The Empress Eugenie, in an act of extraordinary humanity, interceded with the Queen to prevent any recriminations against the man who abandoned her son. Victoria wrote to the review body. When the proceedings of the court-martial were published on 16 August, the adjutant-general stated that the case against Carey was not proven, and that he was relieved of all consequences of the trial. He was ordered back to his regiment, where he was condemned by his fellow officers to live in perpetual Coventry. He died six years later in India.

The whole lamentable episode was from first to last, as the Duke of Cambridge wrote to Lord Chelmsford, 'inexplicable'.

Chapter eleven
Ulundi

On the night of 3 June, the 2nd Division was encamped at the junction of the Ityotyosi and Tombokala Rivers, near where the prince had fallen, with Wood's column three miles away. Buller, scouting ahead of the advancing columns with the Frontier Light Horse, had located a force of some 300 Zulus to the east of the Flying Column, in an area where several kraals had been destroyed. At 4.30am on the 5th, General Marshall led a squadron of the King's Dragoon Guards and another of the 17th Lancers out to disperse them. The Zulus retired into thick bush on a hillside, where the cavalry, unable to manoeuvre, returned the enemy fire dismounted. It was a profitless exchange, and Marshall ordered a retirement. As he did so, Lieutenant Frith, adjutant of the 17th Lancers, was killed. His body, slung across his saddle, and several wounded were all that Marshall had to show for the encounter.

On 4 June, while at the Flying Column's camp on the Nodweni River, Chelmsford received three messengers from Cetewayo. The Zulu king – desperate at the implacable advance of the British columns, the burning of kraals and continued loss of cattle, yet quite unable to check his warriors' enthusiasm for war – had made several unsuccessful attempts to contact Chelmsford. His envoys, uncertain whom to approach and in which column, were invariably turned away as spies. Now, Cetewayo wanted to know why war was waged upon him – a rhetorical question – and more important, what he must do to halt the British advance. Chelmsford replied that he would require all rifles and the two guns taken at Isandhlwana, the laying down of arms by several regiments, and at least 10,000 cattle. After discussion, he modified this demand to the return of all British equipment, the oxen then at Ulundi, and the surrender of a single regiment. The messengers departed with these terms, after informing Chelmsford that there was a European trader with Cetewayo at Ulundi.

By 6 June, the two columns were twenty-five miles from the Blood River, and nearly forty from their base at Koppie Allein. It now became essential to pause and establish a supply depot. On the Nodweni River, therefore, a stone-built and fortified post was constructed, and named Fort Newdigate, after the 2nd Division's commander. This was garrisoned by two companies of the 2nd/21st, with two Gatlings, a squadron of the dragoons, and a NNC company. Then, on the 7th, while the 2nd Division moved on to the Upoko River, over 600 wagons were sent back to Koppie Allein to bring up fresh supplies of food, ammunition and other requirements. The magnitude of this task is underlined by the fact that the wagons were escorted by the entire Flying Column.

By 17 June, the vast convoy was back, enabling the advance to be resumed, but in the interval Lord Chelmsford had received a private letter from Colonel Stanley, the Secretary of State for War, intimating that he, the general, was to be superseded.

The government, unable to understand the slowness with which the second campaign had been mounted, was alarmed at the spiralling cost of the war and could see no rapid end to the conflict. When hostilities did cease, a peace settlement would have to be imposed upon Zululand. There were other areas of native unrest; Sekukuni, a powerful chieftain, was up in arms. In the Transvaal, the disaffected Boers were in a state of incipient revolt. Confederation seemed as remote a possibility as ever, and in the face of these problems it was evident that the civil and military authorities in South Africa were failing to co-operate harmoniously. Chelmsford was more or less at loggerheads with Bulwer, and Wood had crossed swords with Colonel Owen Lanyon, the Administrator of the Transvaal. Frere, upon whom the government's hopes had been pinned, seemed impotent.

In London, therefore, it appeared that the only solution was to appoint an officer to take supreme civil and military command in South Africa, to whom Chelmsford, Frere and Bulwer would all be subordinate. The man chosen was Lieutenant-General Sir Garnet Wolseley, the most outstanding soldier-administrator of his day. The decision was announced in England on 26 May and Wolseley reached Cape Town on 23 June.

News of the appointment, which preceded the official notifications to Frere and Chelmsford, came by a Reuter's telegram, so adding insult to injury. To Chelmsford in particular it was a cruel blow, and seemed timed to deprive him of the fruits of victory. The wording of Stanley's official message, when it finally reached him a month later, after the battle of Ulundi, did little to ameliorate this feeling:

Her Majesty's Government had determined to send out Sir Garnet Wolseley as administrator in that part of South-Eastern Africa in the neighbourhood of the seat of war with plenary powers both civil and military. Sir Bartle Frere instructed accordingly by Colonial Office. The appointment of a senior officer is not intended as a censure on yourself, but you will, as in ordinary course of service, submit and subordinate your plans to his control.

Chelmsford had assumed that he enjoyed the government's confidence. Recall or supersession after Isandhlwana would have been explicable, but now, after countless set-backs, he was upon the verge of final victory, in which lay his only chance of re-establishing his military reputation. Ulundi lay only forty miles away. Chelmsford resolved to push on as fast as his columns were able, before Wolseley could come up with him.

By 28 June, the day Wolseley landed at Durban to begin his journey into Zululand, the Field Force was encamped on the hills of Entonjaneni, from where Ulundi was visible sixteen miles ahead beyond the White Umfolozi. Here Chelmsford received Cetewayo's reply to his peace terms, in the form of a letter written by the white trader, one Cornelius Vyn, whom the original messengers had said was with the king. Cetewayo requested that Chelmsford's troop 'must go back again to home', promised to send the oxen and the two guns, but denied that his warriors had possession of any British rifles. He also sent two 'elephant horns' as proof of his sincerity. For his own part, Vyn explained that he was short of paper and ink, and asked that some might be sent him. Chelmsford sent the Zulu envoys back again, insisting on compliance with his original terms, and stating that he would continue to advance on Ulundi until they were met.

On the hills at Entonjaneni, Chelmsford formed a strong defensive position, consisting of two wagon redoubts and a cattle laager, in which he would leave all transport and impedimenta not absolutely essential for the final push to Ulundi. The post was garrisoned by two companies of the 1st/24th, sixty colonial volunteers, 100 Kaffirs of the NNC and sixty mounted Basutos – 400 rifles in all – plus those medically unfit for the coming march and battle, and some forty European wagon conductors.

On the morning of the 30th, the rest of the Flying Column and the 2nd Division marched out towards the White Umfolozi, flowing below them across a wide sandy plain covered with thorn bushes. The men carried no tents or personal kit, and consequently spent an uncomfortable night on the plain. A single narrow track ran towards the river, ten miles away, and along this some 200 wagons trundled in single file, bearing ten days' supply of food, ammunition, entrenching tools and medical supplies. As the Field Force left the heights around Entonjaneni, telescopes revealed three powerful Zulu columns leaving the royal kraal and marching in the direction of the Umfolozi and towards Chelmsford's little army. Their strength was difficult to determine, but it appeared that the passage of the river would be disputed.

Late the following morning two messengers from Cetewayo presented themselves to Chelmsford with the sword taken from the Prince Imperial and a final message written by Cornelius Vyn:

Message from Zulu King
to Lord Chelmsford Genl.
30th June, 1879

The King called me this morning to write this letter to your worship General Lord Chelmsford.

He brings with a dager as has belonged to the Prins of England [the Prince Imperial's sword] (so they say I do not know of course).

Tomorrow morning the two 7-pounder guns and a lot of oxen will leave tomorrow morning to bring at your worship's feet.

For Cetewayo
C. Vyn   Trader

Sir,

PS. If the English armee is in want for the country, please do me a favour to call for me by bearer that I might get out of the country. I went into the country to bring cattle for blankets and be

Your obedient servant
C.V.

PS. Be strong if the King send his armee. They are about 20,000

Your obedient servant,
C.V.

To this message Lord Chelmsford replied that he was willing to accept 1,000 rifles in lieu of the surrender of a regiment, plus the oxen and the two guns; that he would advance to the river in order that his troops might drink; but that he would delay his further advance until 3 July to give Cetewayo time to comply.

At 1.30 on 1 July the Flying Column reached the bank of the White Umfolozi just as the *impi* was nearing the far side. Wood, anticipating an immediate attack, at once formed square, while the 2nd Division, following a mile behind with the wagons, hastily went into laager. The Zulus, however, withdrew without attempting to cross the river.

The following morning the 2nd Division joined the Flying Column and another fortified position was formed, consisting of a double laager surrounded by a ditch, with a stone-built redoubt on a nearby piece of higher ground. Throughout the day watering parties were harassed by Zulu snipers concealed in the bush on rising ground beyond the river.

By noon on the 3rd no reply had been received from Cetewayo, and Chelmsford knew that the final collision could not be long postponed, for the royal kraal lay only a day's march away. While the defences of the final laager were further improved, Buller and the mounted volunteers were ordered out to discover the nature of the ground upon which the battle of Ulundi would be fought. At 1.30 the mounted men forded the Umfolozi and made for the low hills from which the Zulu riflemen had commanded the river bank. Baker's Horse flushed thirty or forty warriors from the rocks, most of whom they killed with dismounted fire. Buller, with the rest of the volunteer units, rode towards Ulundi, across the Mahlabatini plain, on which the thorn bushes bordering the river gave way to long grass.

After about three miles, when they were within less than a mile of the Zulu capital, Buller's force came across a party of Zulus herding goats, and one particularly massive warrior seemed loath to retire. Captain Lord William Beresford, Wood's staff officer, who had attached himself to the volunteers for the reconnaissance, rode at the man headlong. Archibald Forbes described the encounter:

Bill steadied his horse a trifle, just as he was wont to do before the take off for a big fence; within striking distance he made him swerve a bit to the left – he had been heading straight for the Zulu as if he meant to ride him down. The spear flashed out like the head of a cobra as it strikes; the sabre carried at point, one' clashed with it and seemed to curl around it; the spear head was struck aside; the horseman delivered 'point two' . . . and lo! in the twinkling of an eye the sabre's point was through the shield and half its length buried in the Zulu's broad chest.

Beresford, a keen pig-sticker, cried, 'First spear by Jove!' and rejoined the rest of the force. Hardly had he done so than a tremendous volley crashed out from the long grass, from which a Zulu regiment emerged, estimated at about 4,000 strong, moving rapidly to encircle the horsemen.

As the mounted men turned to retreat, a trooper named Pearce fell dead from his saddle. Sergeant Fitzmaurice, of the 24th, attached to the mounted infantry, fell wounded, as his horse stumbled. The leading Zulus were almost upon him when Beresford and Sergeant O'Toole, of the Frontier Light Horse, turned back. Fitzmaurice was a big man, dazed with the fall and his wound, and it took the combined efforts of both men to heave him on to Beresford's horse. Twice, before they reached the river, Fitzmaurice's dead weight dragged Beresford from his saddle.

When another trooper, one Raubenheim, fell wounded, Commandant D'Arcy, of the Frontier Light Horse, galloped back, controlling his mount with difficulty, and injured his back in the effort of pulling Raubenheim up. His gallant attempt failed, for the Zulus were only a few yards away, and he was obliged to drop the wounded man. Raubenheim's body was found the next day, castrated and disembowelled, with the right hand and nose cut off.

A force of infantry and two 9-pounders had been sent out in support of the reconnaissance. Buller succeeded in withdrawing to the Umfolozi for the loss of three killed and four wounded, but with the information Chelmsford required in order to make his dispositions for the next day.

The British spent a comfortless night in their laager. It was cold and a mist rose from the river; from beyond it came the incessant chanting and throbbing of drums as the Zulu regiments were doctored in preparation for battle.

The troops were quietly roused at 4am on the morning of 4 July, although reveille was not sounded until 5.15 to avoid alerting the Zulus. Buller's men were across the Umfolozi by six o'clock. Except for five companies of the 1st/24th, left to guard the laager under the command of Colonel Bellairs, the deputy adjutant-general, the rest of the Field Force, with a protective screen of horsemen, was on the far bank by seven. Here they were formed into square. The British infantry companies formed the wall, with the Gatlings and field guns placed at intervals around the sides and at the corners. The NNC, ammunition wagons, engineers and bandsmen, soon to act as stretcher bearers, were drawn up within the square, while around it rode the cavalry.

When all was arranged to Chelmsford's satisfaction, the ponderous formation moved slowly off to the north-east with colours flying and the bandsmen playing regimental marches, in the direction of the area Buller had marked the previous day as a suitable position. This was a piece of rising ground set in the Mahlabatini plain, not commanded from any direction, and free from any cover except long grass. On reaching the selected point, the square wheeled half right to face Ulundi, a mile and a half to the east, and halted to await the expected onslaught.

It was by now after eight o'clock, and the sun was well up over the hills that rimmed the plain to the east. The British square, containing only 4,000 red-coats and 1,100 Kaffirs, seemed to young 'Chops' Mossop '. . . a little red matchbox about to be trampled to dust'. The singing of the birds could be heard, as some of the artillerymen took the range of a solitary euphorblia tree, 2,000 yards away on a ridge. Of the Zulu *impi* there was no sign; the only movement on the plain was that of the horsemen spreading out from the square.

Buller and the Frontier Light Horse crossed a small stream known as the Mbilane, and as if that movement had been an awaited sign, the great *impi* suddenly arose from the grass, the regiments, in masses fifty deep, strung out in a vast arc from east to west. The Zulus advanced at a walk and in silence, the horns of the *impi* reaching out to completely encircle the equally silent British square and close their line of retreat. Between the contracting circle and the square the horsemen stood, each trooper facing the enemy. To one eyewitness* at least, it seemed '. . . that the black line has but to tighten and then, with a rush and a bound as it springs into action, overwhelm that small body of British soldiers'.

One by one the Zulu regiments broke into a run. Vyn's estimate was an accurate one: there were about 20,000 warriors in the swiftly tightening ring, representing all the regiments of the Zulu army. The Ngobamakosi were there, and the uVe and the Mbonambi, who had fought so hard against Durnford's men at Isandhlwana; the umCityu, Nokenke, and Ukhandempemvu, who that same day had broken through the centre of the line and wiped out the British infantry; the inDlu-yengwe, uThulwana and the uDoko, who had hurled themselves hour after hour on to the barricades at Rorke's Drift. These were the men who had done battle with Pearson at the Inyezane; or so nearly trapped Buller's force on Hlobane; or served in the great *impi* that had attacked Kambula, or thrown themselves at Chelmsford's laager at Gingihlovu. All, except those still unblooded, had experienced the terrible effect of British volley firing, and the devastation wrought by the guns, but they came on once more, their ferocious courage unquenched. They were in full panoply of war, a moving wall of black picked out with regimental shield colours, and the gleam of assegai blades matching the glint of steel now ringing the red square.

* Mitford, B. *Through the Zulu Country, 1883*, quoting a report in the *Port Elizabeth Telegraph*, 12 August 1879.

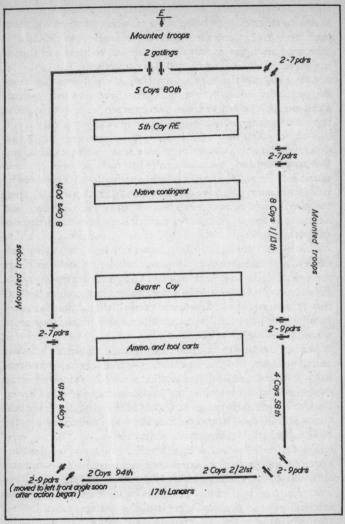

E

Mounted troops

2 gatlings

2-7 pdrs

5 Coys 80th

5th Coy RE

8 Coys 90th

2-7 pdrs

Native contingent

8 Coys 1/13th

Mounted troops

Mounted troops

Bearer Coy

2-7 pdrs

2-9 pdrs

Ammo. and tool carts

4 Coys 94th

4 Coys 58th

2-9 pdrs
(moved to left front angle soon
after action began)

2 Coys 94th

2 Coys 2/21st

2-9 pdrs

17th Lancers

12 The British square at Ulundi

The horsemen retired slowly, lingering until the last moment to fire into the advancing tide of Zulus, goading them to increase their pace and come to close quarters with the waiting infantry. The warriors began beating their assegais against their shields and shouting. The mounted troops retired within the still silent square. Chelmsford and his staff remained on horseback, risking the possibility of being shot, in order to gain a clear view over the heads of the infantry, who were drawn up four deep, with the front two ranks kneeling.

The field guns opened the battle, firing shrapnel and cutting down the Zulus in swathes. The pace of the *impi* increased, and the British infantry battalions began to fire volleys; the clatter of the Gatlings added to the swelling noise and to the gathering pall of smoke around the square. The lines of warriors swept forward, only to disintegrate before the volume of fire; and Zulus leaped over the bodies of their dead or wounded comrades in the effort to come hand to hand with their adversaries, and to match spear against bayonet. Once or twice they nearly succeeded, and there was a bad moment when two of the Gatlings jammed. But it was Kambula and Gingihlovu all over again. Flesh and blood animated by a fanatical courage could not overcome the weapons of science, and the British position remained inviolate, while around it bodies littered the ground ever more thickly.

Within the small red square was a scene of intense activity. Lord Chelmsford rode around giving orders. The surgeons were busy with the wounded. The Kaffirs of the NNC cowered in the centre, still in mortal terror of their enemies. Archibald Forbes, who had lost a £100 bet he had staked earlier that morning that there would be no battle, took notes; while Melton Prior, the *Illustrated London News* artist, made sketches.

For three quarters of an hour the Zulu rushes continued unabated, but at last the decimated regiments began to waver, and their resolution to falter. Chelmsford sensed this and ordered the 17th Lancers to mount. Their colonel, Drury-Lowe, was knocked off his horse by a spent bullet, as he assembled his regiment at the rear of the square, and was momentarily stunned. He rapidly recovered, remounted, and led his troopers out through a gap made between two of the infantry companies.

'Go at them Colonel, but don't pursue too far!' shouted Chelmsford, and raised his helmet to the men.

The 17th Lancers – the Duke of Cambridge's Own – were a proud regiment. 'Death or Glory' was their motto, and Balaclava was amongst their battle honours. Drury-Lowe drew them up meticulously, as if on parade. To Mossop, watching the troopers on their big English horses, with their blue uniforms and white facings, they appeared a machine, so precise was their dressing. Drury-Lowe advanced his regiment at the walk in columns of troops, and, as the ground levelled, gave the orders: 'Trot – Form squadrons – Form line!' Then, with the men drawn up two deep, 'Gallop!' The horses leapt forward, and as the line of steel-tipped lances came to the rest, pennons streaming, 'Charge!' and a cheer broke from the square. The regiment rapidly overtook the retreating Zulus, and the lances, as unsparing as the assegais, rose and fell as the troopers impaled warrior after warrior, and flicked the bodies from the points. As the charge lost momentum, the lances were returned to the sling and sabres drawn; a *mêlée* of individual fights developed. Captain the Honourable Wyatt-Edgell was shot dead and several men were wounded. Then the squadron of dragoons swept by with the mounted volunteers to continue the pursuit, led by the redoubtable Buller, now brandishing an assegai. The Kaffirs of the NNC, their courage restored by the sight of the enemy in full flight, searched out and slew the wounded, and those who failed to retreat quickly enough.

The square broke up, and the troops, after a meal by the side of the Mbilane, marched back to the laager on the Umfolozi. The battle of Ulundi had cost the British twelve killed and eighty-eight wounded. It was, as always, impossible to form an accurate estimate of the Zulu casualties, but between 1,000 and 1,500 lay dead upon the field. The mounted men rode on to Ulundi, to find Cetewayo gone and the great kraal deserted. The 1,500 huts were put to the torch and, as the riders retired, the smoke swept over the Zulu dead on the now deserted Mahlabatini plain.

The Zulu war was now over, as far as Chelmsford was concerned. After spending the 5th in camp on the White Umfolozi, the 2nd Division marched back to the laager on the hills of Entonjaneni, and here, while the troops dismantled the defences, the general wrote his letter of resignation. Mentally and physically exhausted, and still smarting under the insult of supersession, Chelmsford was satisfied with having vindicated himself at Ulundi; for the tiresome task of pacifying the north of the country and arranging a peace settlement, he had no taste. Wolseley was welcome to the job.

Unable to reach the 2nd Division in time for Ulundi, Wolseley had joined Crealock's 1st Division on the coast on 7 July. Chelmsford, sending the 2nd Division back to Fort Newdigate, took the Flying Column towards the coast via St Pauls, where he and Wolseley met on the 16th. From here Chelmsford returned to Pietermaritzburg by way of the Lower Drift, and on 27 July sailed from Durban, bound for England. His reception there was mixed. The Queen bestowed the Order of the Bath upon him, and invited him to Balmoral. Disraeli, about whose ears the Isandhlwana disaster had unleashed a pack of troubles, refused to see him privately, but only officially, at Downing Street. Chelmsford was never offered a command again.

Wolseley, however, could not regard the war as quite finished. The northern part of Zululand was not subdued and, most important of all, Cetewayo was still at large. Two small columns were organised, under Lieutenant-Colonel Clark, 57th Regiment, and Lieutenant-Colonel Russell, 13th Hussars, and despatched to scour Zululand for the king. The rest of the Field Force fell back towards Natal. By late September there were no British troops left in Zululand, and by Christmas none in Natal, apart from the garrisons. The Natal Native Contingent and the mounted volunteers were disbanded and sent back to their homes.

After a prolonged and exhausting hunt, Cetewayo was at last run to ground by a squadron of the King's Dragoon Guards under Major Marter at a kraal named Kwa Dwasa, in northern Zululand. He was exiled to Cape Town. In 1882, now wearing European clothes, he went to England and took a house in Kensington. His popularity was immense. The Queen invited him to luncheon at Osborne, and when he went out in London large and enthusiastic crowds gathered to see the last and bloodthirsty despot of Zululand. In 1883 he returned to his depleted kingdom, where he died in February of the following year.

The Zulu War had cost the British Government – dragged into conflict against its will and indeed against its express instructions – £5,250,000, a sum vastly in excess of expectations. The Army suffered 1,326 dead and wounded, besides one of the worst disasters in its history. The object of the war – the destruction of the Zulu military system – had been achieved, but perhaps it is significant that none of the major figures in the episode emerged with enhanced reputations.

The real tragedy of the war lay not in the fact that it was fought at all – for the fact that the *impis* were a permanent and serious menace to their neighbours is undeniable – but that the fruits of conquest were thrown away in the peace settlement imposed by Wolseley. Had Zululand been annexed to the Crown, and administered as other such territories were, the country might have enjoyed a period of tranquillity and economic growth. But the government was unwilling to assume fresh territorial responsibilities. Wolseley, more with an eye to ensuring that the Zulus could never again be militarily strong than to giving the nation good government, divided the country into thirteen petty states, and placed over each a chieftain chosen either for his co-operation with the British or his known opposition to Cetewayo. The thirteen chiefs were to be responsible to a British Resident and abide by the conditions to which Cetewayo had supposedly been subject. It was an unfortunate plan and had no chance of success. The restoration of Cetewayo served only to crystallise the growing unrest in Zululand, and the country plunged once again into bloody domestic strife.

Appendices

Appendix A Table Showing Strength of Columns January 1879

	No 1 Col Pearson	No 2 Lt-Col Durnford	No 3 Brevet Col Glyn	No 4 Brevet Col Evelyn Wood	No 5 Col Rowlands	Grand Total
Staff	20	5	20	25	15	85
Artillery (men)	23		132	108		263
Artillery (guns)	4-7 pounders 1 Gatling 2 rocket tubes 1 trough	3 rocket troughs	6-7 pounders 2 rocket troughs	6-7 pounders 2 rocket troughs	1 Krupp gun 2-6 pounder Armstrongs	20 guns 2 rocket tubes 8 rocket troughs
Infantry	1,517	—	1,275	1,502	834	5,128
Cavalry	312	—	320	208	553	1,193
Native Contingent	2,256	3,488	2,566	387	338	9,035
Mounted Natives	—	315	—	—	—	315
Conductors, drivers, foreloopers	622	83	346	48	25	1,910
Oxen	3,128	480	1,507	260	150	10,023
Horses	116	498	49	20	10	803
Mules	121	350	67	123	12	398
Wagons	384	30	220	41	17	977
Carts	24	—	82	5	2	56
Total officers and men	4,750	3,871	4,709	2,278	1,565	17,929

Appendix B

State of South African Field Force, May 1879
General Commanding: Lt-Gen Lord Chelmsford, KCB

1st Division: Maj-Gen H. H. Crealock

1st Brigade: Col Pearson

Corps	Strength	Commanding Officer
2nd/3rd Regiment	8 Companies	Lt-Col Parnell
88th Regiment	6 Companies	Lt-Col Lambert
99th Regiment	8 Companies	Lt-Col Welman

2nd Brigade: Lt-Col Clark

Corps	Strength	Commanding Officer
57th Regiment	8 Companies	Maj Tredennick
3rd/60th Rifles	7 Companies	Capt Tufnell
91st Highlanders	8 Companies	Maj Bruce

Divisional Troops

Corps	Strength	Commanding Officer
Naval Brigade + 3 Guns	795	Commander Campbell
4th Batt NNC	789	Capt Barton
5th Batt NNC	1,107	Commandant Nettleton
John Dunn's Scouts	112	Mr J. Dunn
Mounted Troops	564	Maj Barrow
M/6 RA (6-7 pounders)	160	Maj Sandham
8/7 RA (2-7 pounders)	50	Maj Ellaby
11/7 RA (2-7 pounders)	25	Lieut Lloyd
0/6 RA Amm Col	75	Maj Duncan
30th Coy Royal Engineers	85	Capt Blood

2nd Division: Maj-Gen Newdigate

1st Brigade: Col Glyn

Corps	Strength	Commanding Officer
2nd/21st Regiment	6 Companies	Maj Hazlerigg
58th Regiment	6 Companies	Maj Whitehead

2nd Brigade: Col Collingwood

Corps	Strength	Commanding Officer
1st/24th Regiment	7 Companies	Maj Tongue
94th Regiment	6 Companies	Lt-Col Malthus

Divisional Troops

Corps	Strength	Commanding Officer
N/5 RA (6-7 pounders)	150	Lt-Col Harness
N/6 RA (6-9 pounders)	150	Maj Le Grice
O/6 RA Amm Col	68	Capt Alexander
2nd Coy RE	55	Capt Courtney
Mounted Troops*	210	—
2nd Battalion NNC	900	Maj Bengough
AS Corps	150	—
AMD	46	—

The Cavalry Brigade (attached to 2nd Division)
Maj-Gen Marshall

Regiment	Strength	Commanding Officer
1st Dragoon Guards	634	Col H. Alexander
17th Lancers	613	Col Drury-Lowe
Natives attached	108	—

* Bettington's Natal Horse and Shepstone's Basutos.

Brig-Gen Wood's Flying Column

Corps	Strength	Commanding Officer
1st/13th Regiment	617	Maj England
80th Regiment	373	Maj Tucker
90th Regiment	654	Maj Rogers, VC
11/7 RA (4 7-pounders)	81	Maj Tremlett
10/7 RA Gatlings	64	Maj Owen
5th Company RE	82	Capt Jones
Mounted Infantry	95	Capt Browne
Frontier Light Horse	209	Commandant D'Arcy
Transvaal Rangers	77	Commandant Raaf
Baker's Horse	202	Commandant Baker
Natal Native Horse	117	Capt Cochrane
Natal Native Pioneers	104	Capt Nolan
Natal Light Horse	84	Commandant Whalley
Wood's Irregulars	485	Commandant White

Appendix C

Garrisons and Posts of the Line of Communication

Garrison or Post	Corps	Strength
Durban	58th Regiment	1 Company
	Indian Corps	1 Company
Stanger	Various	½ Company approx
Lower Tugela Forts	Various	3 or 4 Companies & Naval Brigade
Pietermaritzburg	2nd/21st Regiment	2 Companies
	General Depot	Variable
Greytown	94th Regiment	2 Companies
Krantz Kop and various outposts	Natal Native Contingent	2 Battalions
Dundee	2nd/24th Regiment	4 Companies
Helpmakaar and Rorke's Drift	2nd/24th Regiment	4 Companies
Ladysmith	58th Regiment	1 Company
Utrecht	2nd/24th Regiment	4 Companies
Newcastle		1 Company
Balte Spruit		1 Company
Luneberg		1 Company
Conference Hill	King's Dragoon Guards	2 Squadrons
	2nd/4th Regiment	1 Company

Appendix D

Isandhlwana, 22 January 1879

Units Engaged and Casualties

Corps or Department	Engaged Officers	NCOs and Men	Killed Officers	NCOs and Men
Staff	3	9	2	9
N/5 Royal Artillery (2-7 pounders)	2	70	1	61
Royal Artillery, 2 rocket tubes	1	9	1	6
Royal Engineers	1	4	1	4
5 Companies 1st/24th Regiment	16	403	16	400
1 Company 2nd/24th Regiment	5	178	5	178
Army Service Corps	—	3	—	3
Army Hospital Corps	1	10	1	10
Army Medical Department	1	1	1	1
Mounted Infantry	—	30	—	13
Natal Mounted Police	—	33	—	26
Natal Carbineers	2	27	2	20
Newcastle Mounted Rifles	2	15	2	5
Buffalo Border Guard	1	8	—	3
Sîkali's Horse, 5 troops	5	257	1	—
1st/1st Regiment NNC	6	240	2	10
1st/3rd Regiment NNC	10	200	8	29
2nd/3rd Regiment NNC	10	200	9	28
No. 1 Coy Natal Native Pioneer Corps	1	10	Not known	Not known
Total:	67	1,707	52	806

Note: The NNC casualties represent Europeans only. 471 natives were also killed, bringing the grand total to 52 officers and 1,277 other ranks.

Appendix E

Rorke's Drift, 22 January 1879

Lieut Chard, RE, Commanding

Regiment or Department	Officers	NCOs and Men	Remarks
Staff	—	1	
Royal Artillery	—	4	3 were sick
Royal Engineers	1	1	
3rd Buffs	—	1	
1st/24th Regiment	—	11	5 were sick
2nd/24th Regiment	1	98	17 were sick
90th Regiment	—	1	Sick
Commissariat Department	3	1	
Army Medical Department	1	3	
Chaplain's Department	1	—	
Natal Native Police	—	3	All sick
Natal Native Contingent	1	6	6 men sick
Ferryman	—	1	
Total:	8	131	35

Total effective: 104 including officers

Casualties

Regiment or Department	Killed Officers	NCOs and Men	Wounded Officers	NCOs and Men	Remarks
1st/24th Regiment	—	3	—	2	1 man died of wounds
2nd/24th Regiment	—	8	—	5	1 man died of wounds
Commissariat Department	—	1	Mr Dalton	—	
Natal Native Police	—	1	—	—	
NNC	—	2	—	2	
Total:	—	15	1	9	

Appendix F Casualties During the Campaign

Action	Engaged		Killed		Wounded		Remarks
	Officers	NCOs and Men	Officers	NCOs and Men	Officers	NCOs and Men	
Inyezane	95	2,687	2	8	1	15	1 man died of wounds
Isandhlwana	67	1,707	52	806	—	—	471 natives also killed
Rorke's Drift	8	131	—	15	1	9	33 men were sick 2 men died of wounds
Intombi	106 of all ranks		2	60	—	1	2 European wagon conductors and 15 native drivers were killed
Hlobane	1,325 all ranks		15	79	1	7	One officer, Captain Potter, was missing Exact numbers of killed in Wood's Irregulars and Mounted Infantry not known
Kambula	2,086 all ranks		—	18	8	57	88 were sick in hospital 10 died of wounds
Gingihlovu	3,390 all ranks		—	4	6	39	2,280 natives also present 4 of the wounded also died
Ulundi	122	2,159	2	10	19	69	465 natives and 108 camp followers present
Minor actions	—	—	3	7	1	9	Includes Prince Imperial
Total:	—	—	76	1,007	37	206	

Table shows number of British troops concerned.
Between 11 January 1879 and 15 October 1879, 17 officers and 330 men died of diseases consequent on the campaign. 99 officers and 1,286 other ranks were invalided for causes incidental to the campaign.

Bibliography

Adams, J. *The South Wales Borderers* (1968)

Arthur, Sir G. (ed), *The Letters of Lord and Lady Wolseley, 1870–1911* (1922)

Ashe, Maj and Wyatt-Edgell, E. V. *The Story of the Zulu Campaign* (1880)

Atkinson, C. T. *The South Wales Borderers, 24th Foot, 1689–1937* (Cambridge 1937)

Binns, C. T. *The Last Zulu King. The Life and Death of Cetewayo* (1963)

Blake, R. *Disraeli* (1966)

Bryant, A. T. *A History of the Zulu and Neighbouring Tribes* (Cape Town 1964)

   Olden Times in Zululand and Natal (Cape Town 1929)

   The Zulu People: As They were Before the White Man Came (Pietermaritzburg 1949)

Bulpin, T. V. *Shaka's Country* (Cape Town 1952)

Butler, L. *Sir Redvers Buller* (1909)

Clements, W. H. *The Glamour and Tragedy of the Zulu War* (1936)

Colenso, F. E. and Durnford, Lt-Col E. *The Ruin of Zululand: an account of British Doings in Zululand Since the Invasion of 1879* (1884)

Coupland, Sir R. *Zulu Battlepiece* (1948)

DeKiewiet, C. W. *The Imperial Factor in South Africa* (Cambridge 1937)

Devitt, N. *Galloping Jack. Being the Reminiscences of Brigadier-General Robinson Royston* (1937?)

Durnford, Lt-Col E. *A Soldier's Life and Work in South Africa, 1872 to 1879. A Memoir of the Late Colonel A. W. Durnford, Royal Engineers* (1882)

Faye, C. *Zulu References* (Pietermaritzburg 1923)

Forbes, A. *Memories and Studies of War and Peace* (1895)
 Barracks, Bivouacs and Battles (1897)

Fortescue, Sir J. W. *A History of the 17th Lancers* (1895)

French, Maj G. *Lord Chelmsford and the Zulu War* (1939)

Furneaux, R. *The Zulu War: Isandhlwana and Rorke's Drift* (1963)

Fynn, A. F. *The Diary of Henry Francis Fynn* (ed Stuart, J. and Malcolm, D. M., Pietermaritzburg, 1950)

Gardiner, A. F. *Narrative of a Journey to the Zoolu Country in South Africa* (1836)

Gibson, J. Y. *The Story of the Zulus* (1911)

Goodfellow, C. F. *Great Britain and South African Confederation, 1870–1881* (Cape Town 1966)

Grant, J. *British Battles on Land and Sea*, 4 (1894)

Haggard, H. Rider. *Cetywayo and his White Neighbours* (1896)

Hallam-Parr, Capt H. *A Sketch of the Kaffir and Zulu Wars* (1880)

Hamilton-Browne, Col G. *A Lost Legionary in South Africa* (nd)

Harrison, Gen Sir R. *Recollections of a Life in the British Army During the Latter Half of the 19th Century* (1908)

Hattersley, A. F. *Carbineer. The History of the Royal Natal Carbineers* (Aldershot 1950)

Hicks Beach, Lady Victoria. *Life of Sir Michael Hicks Beach* (1932)

Holt, H. P. *The Mounted Police of Natal* (1913)

Hook, H. 'How They Held Rorke's Drift', *The Royal Magazine* (February 1905)

John, K. *The Prince Imperial* (1939)

Krige, E. J. *The Social System of the Zulus* (Johannesburg 1936)

Lucas, T. J. *The Zulus and the British Frontiers* (1879)

Ludlow, Capt W. R. *Zululand and Cetewayo* (1882)

Lugg, H. C. *Historic Natal and Zululand* (Pietermaritzburg 1949)

Mackinnon, J. P. and Shadbolt, S. *The South African Campaign* (1879, 1880)

Martineau, J. *The Life and Correspondence of the Rt Hon Sir Bartle Frere* (2 vol, 1895)

Mitford, B. *Through the Zulu Country. Its Battlefields and Its People* (1883)

Molyneux, Maj-Gen W. C. F. *Campaigning in South Africa and Egypt* (1896)

Montague, Capt W. F. *Campaigning in South Africa. Reminiscences of an Officer in 1879* (1880)

Morris, D. R. *The Washing of the Spears* (1966)

Mossop, G. *Running the Gauntlet. Some Recollections of Adventure* (1937)

Norbury, Fleet Surgeon F. *The Naval Brigades in South Africa during the Years 1877–78–79* (1880)

Norris-Newman, C. L. *In Zululand with The British Throughout the War of 1879* (1880)

Rogers, Col H. C. B. *The Mounted Troops of the British Army, 1066–1945* (1945)

   Weapons of the British Soldier (1960)

Smith-Dorrien, Gen Sir H. *Memories of Forty-Eight Years' Service* (1925)

Tisdall, E. E. P. *The Prince Imperial* (1959)

Tomasson, W. H. *With the Irregulars in the Transvaal and Zululand* (1881)

Tylden, Maj G. 'Some Aspects of the Zulu War', *Journal of the Society for Army Historical Research*, 17 (1938)

Verner, Col W. *The Military Life of HRH George, Duke of Cambridge* (2 vol, 1905)

War Office. *Narrative of the Field Operations connected with the Zulu War of 1879–1881* (reprinted 1907)

   Correspondence relative to Military Affairs in South Africa (A.0766)

   Correspondence relative to Military Affairs in Natal and the Transvaal (A.0732)

Whitton, Lt-Col F. E. *Service Trials and Tragedies* (nd)

   'Rorke's Drift', *Blackwood's Magazine* (February 1934)

'Isandhlwana', *The Nineteenth Century and After* (January 1929)

Wilkins, P. A. *The History of the Victoria Cross* (1904)

Williams, C. *The Life of Lieutenant General Sir Henry Evelyn Wood* (1882)

Wilmot, A. *History of the Zulu War* (1880)

Wood, Sir E. *From Midshipman to Field Marshal* (1906)

Worsfold, B. *Sir Bartle Frere. A Footnote to the History of the British Empire* (1923)

Index